Alfred Nawrath Norway

Alfred Nawrath

NORWAY

Robert B. Luce Co., Inc.
Washington – New York

Graphical presentation: Kümmerly & Frey, Geographical Publishers, Berne
Photolithography and printing of colour plates:
Kümmerly & Frey, Graphical Institute, Berne

Printed in Switzerland
ISBN 0-88331-087-2

Published in the United States, 1976

Library of Congress Card Catalog Number 76-17134

Contents

Seal of King Magnus IV, surnamed the 'Law-Mender', known in Norway as Magnus Haakonsson Lagaböter, 1263–1280.

Foreword

This photobook embraces the whole of Norway, from Cape Lindesnes on the skerry-strewn south coast, up to the North Cape, and even beyond to Magdalena Bay on Spitsbergen, only 1,000 kilometres from the North Pole. The photographs were taken in the course of several trips to the north made at various times and at every season of the year. Thus, two of the plates show the bridge across the sea at Tromsö, one in the course of its construction, one after its completion; and anyone who is familiar with the north will notice that the pictures of Spitsbergen, or Svalbard, were taken at the beginning of June and the end of August. In a series of photographs such as this, however, whose numbers must of necessity be limited, it is obviously impossible to reproduce all the outward geographical forms and features of this many-faceted country, and to do full justice to all the aspects of its economy and culture.

A bare three per cent of Norwegian territory, excluding the Arctic regions, is agriculturally exploitable. But the living that is denied the Norwegian by the barren rock of his native soil is accorded him in abundance by the sea to the south, the west, and the north, for, as the poet says:

'...boils the sea in rivers wide
At depths profound about the rocks!'

A book about Norway without a description of its economic backbone, fishing, and its world-wide shipping, would be unthinkable. These subjects are given the attention they deserve. The contributions made by Norway, Sweden, and Finland to the social welfare of the nomad Lapps, the roving aboriginal inhabitants of the extreme north of our continent, have also been considered with due interest and esteem. Norway was largely responsible for the fact that the Lapps were spared the fate of the native inhabitants of some of the other continents.

1 Oslo: Town Hall and training-ship

Without being too rigid in plan, our pictures take the reader from the centre to the periphery, and from south to north. Oslo, the capital, is followed by the great maritime centre, Bergen, the town of Edvard Grieg, and Trondheim, the city founded by Saint Olaf, whose cathedral reflects a marked Anglo-Saxon influence. Norwegian individuality is expressed in the wooden stave churches, three of which, situated at places far apart, are here reproduced. They show high manual skill, workmanship, and artistry, which were not merely isolated phenomena, but a common Norwegian possession. The little shingle-covered wooden churches, which look as if they are wrapped in a scaly dragon's-skin, are strangely reminiscent of Buddhist pagodas. The frequently repeated dragon *motif* is a relic of Viking times, of that pagan epoch which did not lie so very far back when the building of Christian churches began–churches whose ridge-poles and door-jambs were decorated, as were the prows of their famous ships, with dragon's-heads, to ward off tempests and evil spirits.

Let us not, however, anticipate the pleasure of those who will discover Norway here for the first time, nor the joy that the seasoned traveller to the north will experience when he revives his memories of past journeys, and who may perhaps be reminded of much that he had forgotten.

Alfred Nawrath

OVKIII

3

4

5

7

8

From Lindesnes to the North Cape

Viewed from the sea, the Norwegian mainland looks bleak and forbidding, a ponderous, weather-beaten, grey granite massif, washed for thousands of years by the swirling ocean waves, the spray, and the spindrift. In the peaceful waters between the holms of the skerries, sounds and bays come into sight, and in the lee of the cliffs the friendly homes of the sailors and fishermen bid the stranger a hospitable welcome. Here, time seems to stand still, but the well-tended white Norwegian settlements in the outer harbour dream of far-distant days when this most southerly part of the country was covered with oak forests, whose timber meant as much to the ship-builders of those times as do iron and steel to the modern industries of today. From all over Europe timber specialists used to come to southern Norway to buy wood, and this early contact with other countries was one of the basic factors that led to Norway's international prestige in the construction of the sailing-ship of those days, and to the shipping-industry of our own times, one of the main activities within the modern Norwegian economy.

There are no longer any oak forests in the south of the present-day kingdom, and no great sailing-ships weigh anchor in the outer harbour today. The continuity has, however, not been broken. The little town of Farsund, for instance, with a mere few thousand inhabitants, has become the biggest shipping centre, relatively speaking, in the world, thanks to its merchant fleet of a few hundred tons.

Listerland, near the town of Lista, a flat stretch of coast in the extreme south of the country, is a special geographical case and has the appearance of being a prolongation of Denmark's weather-worn coast. It is particularly exposed to tempests and heavy squalls and, during the winter hurricanes, its houses are abandoned to the unleashed elements. When winter is over, however, it is Listerland that receives the first harbingers of spring, before any other region. The flat lowland is suffused with a magical green light from the glittering sea, and above the breath-taking glory of the early flowers, birds of passage glide smoothly in low flight over the peat moors, filling the air with their raucous cries. Yet this spectacle is experienced by only one half of Listerland's population, for the other houses stand empty, awaiting the return of the occupants who have left them. Here we find ourselves face to face with a phenomenon of the poorest and least privileged part of Norway. Though a people of skilled small farmers, for generations many of the inhabitants have emigrated to America to earn a living as manual workers in the great cities of that vast country. They also cross the Atlantic and the North American continent in order to engage in salmon-fishing in the waters of British Columbia. They leave their native homeland on account of the poverty of its soil, and, with open-mindedness and vitality, they adapt themselves to new conditions. The well-ordered little farms of Listerland lie in a sparsely-wooded region, consisting mainly of barren hills, only a bare three per cent of its area being arable land. The 'flight from the land' of the country population experienced all over Europe is also met with here, but there are no towns to which they could migrate. The majority of southern Norwegians have only a very vague notion of Oslo, though well-informed concerning the living-conditions in the huge American cities. Fifty years ago, more than a third of all Norwegians born in Listerland went to live in the United States and sent home thousands of dollars annually, through their native local authorities, to their countrymen in southern Norway. In certain regions, up to 90 per cent of the resident families are supported financially by relatives in the United States and in Canada.

The present dynamic industrial development subjects the face of Norway to constant change, which often takes place so rapidly that, in describing it, one has the feeling that one's pen lags behind events. While the inclemency of Norway's weather used to be a co-determining factor in its poverty, it has apparently also become the cornerstone of its prosperity.

OSLO
STOCKHOLM
HELSINKI
MOSKVA
DUBLIN
KØBENHAVN
LONDON
AMSTERDAM
BERLIN
WARSZAWA
BRUXELLES
PARIS
PRAHA
WIEN
BERN
BUDAPEST
BEOGRAD
BUCUREST
MADRID
LISBOA
ROMA
SOFIJA
TIRANË
ANKARA
ATHINAI
RABAT
ALGER
TUNIS

In certain zones of western Norway, the rain that comes in from the sea amounts to 180 millimetres (over seven inches) per day, and in winter the desolate mountain ridges lie deep in snow. With the onset of the spring thaw, the rivers and lakes swell enormously, and in summer the snow disappears only slowly from the mountains, while the water-level sinks steadily. Without incurring great expense, the achievements of modern technics make it possible to regulate this water by the construction of large dams. By means of the skilful utilization of these natural forces, Norway has become one of the world's leading producers of electric energy.

When we see the deeply-cleft mountains of southern Norway from the air, it is hard to believe that this country is habitable at all. Between rocky peaks, snow-clad slopes, and gleaming glaciers, the snow-free patches often resemble the silhouettes of legendary prehistoric animals; the endless expanses of reindeer-moss, mountain-birches, and pasture-land emerge from the landscape in incredible colours. Out on the west coast, fjords that are hundreds of kilometres in length cut into the interior of the country, where technical development has left its traces, proof that Norway is no longer untouched by modern progress. The construction of dams and power-stations has already wrought drastic transformations in the topographical structure of the country and will inevitably lead to the industrialization of these southern regions.

The abundant supply of electric energy available in Norway has resulted in far-reaching changes in the way of life of its inhabitants, and has not been without effect on the Norwegian community as a whole. Norway, the traditional fishing country, has become a modern industrial nation with a high standard of living and a stable economy. According to recent statistics in the United Nations Year Book, the amount of electricity generated in Norway per head of the population is double that of any other country. Comparative *per capita* figures are as follows: Norway 13,984 kw., Canada 8,103 kw., U. S. A. 6,614 kw., Sweden 6,837 kw., Switzerland 5,033 kw.,—these figures refer to the total amount of electricity consumed. Norway's leading position becomes even more evident when it is considered that the energy is generated exclusively by water-power. Over 98% of the population of Norway, including the remote lateral valleys and the islands off the mainland, is today supplied with electricity, and it was first and foremost small-scale industry that benefited from the abundant supply, though wholesale manufacture is still growing. The construction of power-stations continues, and Nature's former realm is gradually being turned into a gigantic arsenal of technical progress. Large areas of southern Norway, until recently rather neglected step-children of the country, are now thriving, and the little village communities of yesterday are rapidly becoming the industrial centres of tomorrow.

Going from south to north, the first large town on the west coast of Norway is Stavanger, one of the country's most progressive centres, with broad streets and new buildings, especially in the districts where the shipping companies have their offices. Its modern shipyards, with a dock capacity of as much as 80,000 tons, enjoy an excellent reputation throughout the world; in the local markets we find the first-class produce of Jaeren, the fertile coastal lowlands below the flat-contoured hills south of Stavanger. While the rest of Norway is still lying under a blanket of snow, the country's earliest garden-produce, which is of the finest quality, comes on to the market here in abundance. Holly trees, the last outliers of the evergreen forests of Mediterranean regions, grow in the mild maritime climate of the islands off the coast.

Bergen, the chief town of the 'Fylke' (i.e. province) of Bergen and Hordaland, is the second-largest port, with some 200,000 inhabitants, and assuredly the most lively and beautiful town in the country. In the Middle Ages, the coronation of the Norwegian kings took place here, and Bergen's history stretches far back to pre-Viking times. Later, it slipped away from the Norwegian sphere of influence and fell under Hanseatic rule for three hundred years. Once the mightiest town of the North Sea countries, Bergen now once again plays the rôle of the most significant point of departure for the Seven Seas, and it has remained a patrician town of ancient traditions. Bergen's place of historical interest, Bryggen near Vaagen, is a row of dwelling-houses, business premises, and warehouses, gabled buildings set very close together along the quayside. Owing to the type of construction and the site, the buildings have been ascribed to the Hanseatic period, but they are actually a great deal older. Like all old Norwegian wooden towns, Bergen has repeatedly been the victim of ravaging fires, though its characteristic central area has fortunately not been seriously impaired. It is intended to make of Bryggen a centre of native handicrafts and similar activities. Such names as Edvard Grieg, Björnstjerne Björnson, Henrik Ibsen, and Ludvig Holberg are closely associated with the town of Bergen.

The life of Norway's coastal population has always been hard. In the outer harbours, as winter nears its end, fishermen in their tens of thousands assemble with heavy equipment in anticipation of the herrings which are on their way to the coast. The task of locating the shoals of fish, ascertaining their routes and the exact depth at which they are swimming, is entrusted to research ships in the North Sea. For a long time, herring-fishery was regarded as a gamble with the ocean, upon which the livelihood of a large part of the Norwegian population depended, for the income of the fishermen was limited to their share of the catch. If their nets failed to catch the fish, as was not infrequently the case, a year of privation lay ahead for the people living along the coast. In addition to modern echo-sounding apparatuses, the fishing-boats are equipped with highly efficient drag-nets capable of catching a hundred tons of herring at one cast. Bank loans are an encumbrance that weigh heavily on most of the costly ships, so that a bad year at sea has serious economic consequences. In the first place, about thirty thousand fishermen and their families are hard hit by such a misfortune, but there are also considerable repercussions on the country's entire economy.

The operations of the Norwegian fishermen at sea are carefully organized and planned in advance. The headquarters on the mainland are in constant radio contact with the several thousand ships lying off the coast, and the whole fleet can be ordered at a moment's notice to wherever the herring have been located. In order to enable the fishing-flotilla to catch the fish without a break, supporting units are sent out to take over the haul, for time is precious during the fishing operations, especially in bad weather. Since the herring have resorted to the Norwegian coasts, the number of big ocean-going steamers has been reduced, and increased importance is now attached to coastal vessels. On a clear day, the sight of this armada of commercial units is most impressive. In 1955, a record year, the large-scale herring-fishery on the west coast registered a haul of a million tons. The following years, however, were far less favourable and severe economic set-backs ensued. There was a great deal of scientific reflection on the law of averages in the case of herring-fishing, but the phenomenon of its incalculability is not really new.

In earlier times especially, when the Norwegian fishing-fleet was far from having reached the technical level that it has today, the towns on the west coast experienced periods of prosperity or bitter poverty, according to the yield from the sea. For a long time Kristiansund, for example, made a lucrative living from the herring trade; then one day the fish failed to appear, and did not return for many years. Obeying the dictates of necessity, the town sold its fishing-fleet and the entire fishery equipment to Ålesund. Ironically, the herring returned to Kristiansund a few months later.

Fishing with heavy ocean-going vessels equipped with trawl-nets is a far less risky business, and a regular income affords a more solid economic basis. For the Norwegian fishermen, however, the main disadvantage lies in the completely different system of fishing, which means that they must relinquish their standing as free profit-sharing partners, to be relegated to the position of salaried employees in a fishing industry. The development in this direction can, however, hardly be avoided, since the Norwegian Government gives preference to the larger ships, which are independent of the seasons and afford full employment throughout the year, and even in distant waters.

At the extreme end of Trondheim Fjord there is a flat, desolate stretch of lowland with barren peat moors extending down to the sea. But the fjord opens in the direction of the fertile Tröndelag to the town of Trondheim, the legendary Nidaros, steeped in the tradition of the Norwegian Middle Ages. This beautiful town attained a position of significance mainly owing to its Gothic cathedral, a national shrine built over the grave of the Martyr King, St. Olav, who fell fighting for Christianity at the Battle of Stiklestad in 1030. In the present-day Protestant State, the Norwegian kings are crowned in this cathedral, so that it is again invested with some of the dignity that it enjoyed in the Middle Ages. With its mediaeval magnificence, the cathedral was long the most beautiful in northern Europe, but it suffered severe damage at the hands of the Swedish troops during the Scandinavian Seven Years' War, about the middle of the 15th century. When Norway achieved independence in the year 1814, the restoration of the cathedral was begun, a work which is still being faithfully continued today.

At the time of the Trondheim patricians, powerful trading-houses controlled the economy of western Norway and beyond to the Far North. One of the fine mansions recalls the time when Trondheim was the centre of a rich and fertile region along Trondheim Fjord. This late 17th-century wooden building in rococo style today serves as the King's residence when he visits the town.

10 Loshavn, a small harbour on the Lista peninsula
11 Skatöy, in the wide Kragerö Fjord

11▹

12 Heddal in Telemark, largest of Norway's old stave churches
13 Borgund stave church, 12th century
14 Urnes stave church with wooden columns

13

14

16

18

19

20

21

22▷

24

To go to northern Norway, the traveller boards a big modern steamer of the 'Hurtigrute' Line, the journey from Bergen to Kirkenes, on the Russian border, taking five days. On this journey, the ship approaches very close to the Arctic Circle, and the traveller experiences the enthralling drama of the midnight sun. In ancient times, Greeks undertook the first journey to Ultima Thule, that distant land where, in summer, darkness never falls and the sun never sets. According to the geographer Pytheas, he appears to have crossed the North Sea from the Shetland Isles to the Norwegian coast in 300 B.C.

Knut Hamsun wrote a eulogy on the Norwegian summer in his unforgettable 'Pan', and Jonas Lie has compared the endless expanses of his country to the kingdom of Lilliput, with its tiny inhabitants, which Gulliver saw on his travels. Nature is indeed as majestic as the poets would have us believe, but the sight of the departing fishing-fleet, for example, with hundreds of craft of all shapes and sizes, is equally overwhelming. In earlier times, the cod-fishing off the Lofoten Islands was the most extensive in the world, and it was frequently necessary to cover considerable distances in order to reach the fishing-grounds, which often took many days in a rowing-boat. During the heyday of cod-fishing around the Lofoten Islands, up to thirty thousand fishermen took part, among them small farmers who also tilled a little patch of poor land too infertile to afford them an adequate livelihood. The largest catch used to be landed shortly after New Year's Day. Today, the codfish are transferring their spawning-grounds more and more to the west shore of the fjord, where areas of up to forty square kilometres of spawning cod can be located at depths of fifty to a hundred metres.

Tromsö, a harbour-town situated on a northern island in Tromsösund, with a population of 38,000, is both the capital of 'Fylke' Troms and the administrative centre of that extensive northern Norwegian province. Its Natural History Museum, with hydrographical laboratories, merits attention mainly for its activities in the field of oceanography and scientific biological research on fish. In the old days, too, Tromsö used to be the most important point of departure for polar expeditions, and it served as a base for the whaling-fleets operating in the Arctic Ocean. The present-day significance of the town as a whaling-centre is declining, for the whale has been almost exterminated in the northern regions of the Arctic Ocean. Today, whaling is being increasingly replaced by seal-fishery, with Tromsö and other west coast towns as the ports of embarkation. Round about the little island of Jan Mayen and outside the Newfoundland waters, up to three hundred thousand seals are caught annually. The majority of the seventy or so sealing-vessels are stationed in Tromsö harbour.

The closer we approach the Far North, the more striking becomes the change in the scenery. While, until now, the ship has travelled past jagged rock formations often as much as a thousand metres high, the travellers are greeted at the start of the last great stage of the journey, when the ship enters Lopp Havet, by the immensity of Finnmark's wastes, the land of Lapps and reindeer. Extending towards the Arctic Ocean, it embraces, with its 40,000 square kilometres, one-sixth of Norway's territory, thus exceeding Denmark in size. The line of the coast comes into view between the rugged contours of the widely-spaced fjords, some of which are flanked by precipitous mountains.

Finnmark is the home of some 78,000 people, and it is by no means so forbidding as it appears. As far as the unproductive ground permits, the inhabitants engage in agriculture, but fishing is really their main occupation and source of food. The climate is mostly stormy and cold. Arctic plants, heather, and bushes grow on the coast and there are also extensive areas of lichen, while on the upper reaches of the fjords, which are protected from the wind, we find pine-trees and birches. Half the population lives in small towns, where flourishing fishing industries have developed, especially during more recent years. Whereas iron-ore is worked only here and there in the mountains, a small mining-town has sprung up in eastern Kirkenes, not far from the Russian border.

Finnmark was particularly hard hit by the Second World War, and one of Norway's primary post-war duties was the reconstruction of this region, a task which became a symbol of the will to co-operate, and it was the main concern of the Norwegian Government. Twenty-six parishes and three towns have been rebuilt, and all the harbours and distribution centres have been reconstructed. The difficulties entailed in procuring the necessary materials are depicted in an authentic report which states that it would have been easier to build up all these towns in North Africa!

Present-day and pre-war Finnmark differ from each other in many respects, and in this connection the modernization of the fishing industry deserves special mention. A large factory run by the Nestlé concern has not only brought prosperity to what was once the poorest of Norway's provinces, but has also become of equal significance for Europe's fish supply. Finnmark is no longer isolated from the rest of the world; it can be reached by aeroplane today in as many hours as it formerly used to take days. The various regions are linked by motorways and bus routes, and they will soon become centres of modern tourism.

The steep, dark profile of the North Cape, where the sun does not set from the 14th of May to the 30th of July, towers majestically above the waves of the Arctic Ocean. This famous promontory is a fissured massif of grey-black slate, rising to a height of 307 metres (over 1,000 feet), on Mageröy Island. According to the most recent measurements, the western promontory of the island, Knivskjellodden, situated at latitude 71° 11′ 8″ north, is the northernmost point of Norway, while North Kyn, at latitude 71° 8′ 1″ north and longitude 27° 40′ 9″ east, some 38 miles east of the North

Cape, is actually the northernmost point of the European mainland. Not far from the North Cape, and at about the same latitude, there rises the mountain called Hjelsoystauren, inhabited by millions of birds.

After this sketch of Norway's elongated west coast, from Lindesnes (also known as The Naze) via the North Cape to the most northerly Iron Curtain outposts on the Russian border, we turn to the southern parts of the country, with their wooded regions, so much more favoured by Nature. In spite of Norway's predominantly mountainous structure, about 25% of the country's surface is productive woodland, the timber-line for conifers, firs and pinc-trees, which we find everywhere in southern Norway, lying at 800 metres. In view of the relatively unfavourable cultivability of Norwegian land, special significance attaches to forestry. The numerous waterways in the most densely-wooded areas have proved to be a great asset in the exploitation of this region, facilitating as they do the rational floating of the logs to the saw-mills at the river-mouths.

Timber, being a valuable raw material today, is no longer used for heating and building purposes. As well as being employed in the manufacture of cellulose and paper, wood can now be used for the production of artificial silk, a new departure due to modern technical progress. Today, the wood-refining industry represents a good third of the country's export value, and the wood production is expected to double in the course of this generation.

In the most beautiful of the great Norwegian valleys, Gudbrandsdal, three of the famous old stave churches, with their walls of timber boards and their sharply-sloping shingle-covered roofs, have been preserved, thanks to the dry climate. They date back to the time of the introduction of Christianity into Norway in the year 1000, and are regarded as three of the nation's oldest treasures. At the time of the Migration of the Peoples, the Vikings must have returned to Norway from their voyages strongly influenced by other countries in the art of church-building. The majority of the 1,200 churches constructed during the Christian Middle Ages were stave churches, built above all in the valleys, mostly over the sites of old heathen temples. They have several features in common with the Eastern churches, but the intention of their designer was unambiguous—to copy the contemporary Romanesque stone churches in a compact form of wooden architecture, unequalled in beauty anywhere in the world.

A comprehensive idea of the rich cultural tradition of Gudbrandsdal is provided by Anders Sandvig's unique collection of buildings in Lillehammer. Even in the mountain communities of the Telemark district, there is evidence of a masterly style in architecture which reflects that of the Middle Ages. One of its main characteristics is the decorative 18th-century rose-*motif* paintings, virtually a provincial rococo in direct association with the European form of this style.

The old copper-town of Röros, not far from the Swedish border, is unique in structure and in that it is the only town in the high mountains in Norway. Both town and copper-works date from the year 1644, and they have retained their original character intact in spite of devastating fires. The copper-mines at Röros were the most important in the country, with an annual output of 100,000 tons of copper and 500,000 tons of copper-pyrites; today, however, prospecting is coming to an end. Unlike other deserted mining centres all over the world, Röros will not become a ghost-town, for is has been put under State protection and made a cultural centre.

While the raising of Norway's standard of living to the level of that of other European welfare states is commendable, many regret to see the oldest and most deeply-rooted farming community in Europe turning into such a highly industrialized nation. Whereas a hundred years ago, 70% of Norway's population still lived by agriculture, this figure has fallen to 15% today (19% fishery included), and it threatens to decrease still further. The backbone of Norwegian democracy is the peasantry, and their striving for independence in a land which has never known bondage or serfdom is quite legitimate. The only feasible form of democracy for the Norwegian peasant class is that of mutual help and unswerving loyalty among themselves. It was less the Labour movement than the peasantry which generated this fundamentally democratic attitude. While over 90% of all Norwegian farmers are landowners, only 5% are tenant farmers. Their farmsteads are small, but they include some forest-land. Formerly, the possession of woods was considered a stabilizing factor; today it is the *sine qua non* of running a farm with profit.

The really important agricultural regions in the country are situated mainly in the catchment area of Oslo Fjord, in the wide Tröndelag along the interior of Trondheim Fjord, and in the Jaeren area, near Stavanger, on the west coast. It was certainly because Norwegian agriculture felt that its existence was threatened that the dawning crisis was faced so resolutely. Where machine power promised a more rational farm management, agriculture became mechanized. Three thousand State-subsidized machine centres were established for the purpose of affording technical assistance to small farmers. The intensification on the agricultural front is also seen in the production of artificial manure, which has increased five-fold since the Second World War, without permitting the assumption, however, that the country now lives on its own produce as regards bread-stuffs, since only 7% of the nation's requirements is cultivated on Norwegian soil. The emphasis lies on cattle-breeding and dairy-produce, a fact that has resulted in an increase of 15% in the dairy-produce and a simultaneous decrease of 25% in the milk-cow stock, so that there was a surplus of butter and cheese.

Oslo, the capital and administrative centre of Norway, is a venerable old town founded 900 years ago by the Viking leader Harold Hardrada (in Norwegian called Harald

Harderade); today the town has all the aspects of a modern city. There is nothing left to remind the observer of Oslo's originally rural character, shed only in the course of this century—yet Norway's history is clearly reflected in it. The old town with its royal palace, its churches and monasteries, is literally sunk in the earth; ruins dating from the late Middle Ages were brought to light during the building of the railway installations in the eastern part of the town, and a vivid picture of the splendour of the life at the courts of the old Norwegian kings and their entourage is also provided by traditional Norwegian legends. Around the year 1300, unfortunate political constellations led to the country's ruin, to the loss of its independence, and to subjugation by Copenhagen. The epoch of complete passivity, known as 'the 400 years' night', began. During this period, Norway stood in striking contrast to its neighbouring country, Sweden, which was then approaching its zenith as a great European power. It was not a period of celebrated battles but of lethargic indifference, reflected in all spheres of cultural life.

The old Oslo passed away, to be rebuilt as Christiania by King Christian IV at the time of the Renaissance. With the exception of the fortress of Akershus, there is hardly a trace left in present-day Oslo of Christiania's eventful history. To judge by its site and construction, the fortress was built as a typical mediaeval castle by that most ostentatious of all the old Norwegian kings, Haakon V. This magnificent monument has today attained new fame and dignity.

The year 1814 marks the first step leading to modern Norway, a turning-point in the country's more recent history. Napoleon's Continental Alliance with Denmark against England had been concluded mainly at the expense of Norway, which was ceded with the rest of the assets after the bankruptcy due to the Napoleonic Wars, falling to the Swedish Crown Prince, Carl Johan Bernadotte, one of Napoleon's ex-generals, who had gone over to the Emperor's enemies in good time. At

25 In Opland, between Sogne Fjord and Hedmark
26 Valuable raw material: timber on the Sognevatn in Aust-Agdet

this juncture Norway's interests were, for obvious reasons, directed towards England, which was fast bringing economic ruin upon the country by blockading the Norwegian coast. This downfall was all the more painful, as Norway had been hopefully steering towards a brighter future as a flourishing welfare state at the end of the 18th century.

In 1814, a group of Norwegian patriots assembled at the little manor-house of Eidsvoll, north of Oslo, and proclaimed Norway's independence, giving it the most liberal constitution of any European country. Circumstances forced a union with Sweden, but the fundamental principles of Eidsvoll were, nevertheless, put into effect. This union with Sweden lasted until 1905, when Norway broke away from her neighbour and re-instated her own monarchy after a lapse of 600 years. In spite of the gravity of the Norwegian-Swedish conflict, the acute danger of war was banished and an agreement was concluded between the two countries.

When Oslo once again became the capital of the kingdom, it was a provincial town of 10,000 inhabitants. Although it possessed palaces and manor-houses dating from earlier times, the general setting was rather modest for a metropolis. The town had no public life, no theatres, museums, or places of entertainment, and there was not one monument in honour of a great Norwegian. The easy optimism of the golden days of 18th-century mercantilism had given place to the sober realism and unimaginative austerity of the so-called Empire Period. It was in this atmosphere of inertia and stagnating cultural life that the great poet, Henrik Wergeland, appeared. His poetic warmth and vitality filled the little community with faith in the nation's future and awakened a feeling of brotherhood and unity among all classes. Thanks to Wergeland, Norway became aware of the many possibilities inherent in its constitution. He inspired the youth of Norway with courage. He was the spark which fired the artistic and poetic renaissance which was soon to follow.

E-6022
RUTEVOGN

27 Undergrowth at the bottom of a gorge in Norangesdal, between Hellesylt and Oeye
28 Old wooden bridge and water-mill in Ottadal

The two main figures in Norwegian literature were Björnstjerne Björnson and Henrik Ibsen, both of whom gave unsurpassed descriptions of the nation's tendency to vacillate always between hope and despair. Björnson, Wergeland's literary heir, was prone to melancholy rather than to mirth; while his predecessor had eulogized wind, sky, and clouds, Björnson was himself as the germinating earth. He was the teacher and spokesman of his people, often lending his words a faintly political colour. The son of a pastor, he was born in the upper Osterdal (Orkedal) and grew up in the mountainous region of Romsdal, close by the sea. As a young poet he set himself the task of bringing home to the peasant classes their great national heritage and to make them aware of ideas that went beyond the narrow limits of their little world. His work kindled Norwegian self-confidence, which, in view of the continued dissension with Sweden, was soon to become an important political factor.

Ibsen was of a different nature, and it was no wave of national romanticism that led him to write poetry. Before he was twenty years old, and while he was still living in his hometown of Grimstad, he wrote his first drama, Catalina, about the rebel Catiline. This work was not well received and quickly fell into oblivion. His early years in Oslo brought him little success, and he remained practically unknown. However, as he says himself, the vicissitudes of his fortunes were to lead him to see things in their true proportions and he experienced a moment of vision under the impression of St. Peter's in Rome. Inspired by Sören Kjerkegaard, he first wrote, with logical consistency, the great play 'Brand', a tense dramatic work on the power of ethical principles; then 'Peer Gynt', written while he was contemplating a scorpion imprisoned in a jar under the scorching sun of Ischia. These two dramas, so diametrically opposed, led to a catharsis in the poet, so profound that it amounted to a change of personality, with the concomitant phenomena of an inner split.

Ibsen's ambivalent relations with Norway not infrequently appear in the light of a love-hate conflict. In reality, he was unable to free himself from all the painful disappointments he had experienced in his youth, and he left his native country in bitterness for a voluntary exile which was to last for twenty-seven years. In his heart, however, Ibsen was never really able to sever himself completely from the land of his birth, and he constantly refers to Norway in his works. In his later dramas, he lifted the figures in the little Norwegian towns out of their narrow setting and grafted them into the context of the world, where, by reason of their symbolic value, they have become common property. Today, Ibsen's study, with its furniture upholstered in the embossed plush of the 1800's, decorated with a portrait of the great Swedish playwright, August Strindberg, is still preserved in the Norwegian National Museum.

Besides Björnson and Ibsen, the two principal exponents of Norway's literary Golden Age, numerous other poets and artists have taken up the problems of the young State with a growing sense of realism. Arne Garborg, Jonas Lie, and Alexander Kjelland, for example, have written with convincing eloquence on the interests of the various regions of Norway. Norwegian art and literature soon became conceptions which spread beyond the frontiers of the country itself and took root in world culture. The melancholy and mystic Norwegian folk-music of the valleys and the fjords, with its pathos and close association with Nature, which had remained unknown to the outside world for hundreds of years, achieved international fame, not least thanks to the composer Edvard Grieg. Immediately on Ibsen's problematic works followed Knut Hamsun's fascinating poetry on the clear northern nights, and in later years, his great novels, with their disarming directness.

The Nobel prize-winner Sigrid Undset wrote her novels about mediaeval Norway with great historical knowledge and perception. She depicts the fundamental *motifs* of Christian ethics, and her epic portrayal of the social surroundings are unparalleled. Olav Duun's poetical descriptions of the more modern peasant community are of striking analytical penetration.

In the 19th century Norway awoke from her many hundred years of 'twilight sleep'. This awakening took place in many different spheres, one of the most shining examples of the young nation's transition to vigorous activity being given by Fridtjof Nansen of Oslo. At the entrance to the harbour of this town stands an enormous gabled building, which shelters the world's most famous polar ship, the 'Fram', which ventured farther into the immense expanses of the Arctic and the Antarctic than any other vessel. Before he built the 'Fram', Nansen's crossing of Greenland's ice on skis had brought him world-wide fame as a polar explorer. He endeavoured to prove scientifically that the Arctic Ocean could actually be traversed by ship if only the vessel were of adequately robust construction, so that it could resist the pressure of the ice and in this way not be lifted by the ice-floes. For three years, Nansen sailed the northernmost Arctic Ocean in the 'Fram', coming closer to the North Pole than anyone before him. He and his companions left their ship and attempted to reach the Pole on skis and with dog-sleds, getting as far as latitude 84° 14′ north. The trek through the ice-wastes lasted one whole year, which obliged the explorers to winter there. The dauntless audacity of this classic performance deserves our great admiration.

Nansen also played a significant rôle as a politician in Norway's more recent history. He was his country's spokesman in its dealings with the Great Powers during the crisis with Sweden, and his humanitarian activities after the First World War put him in the limelight of the world events of that time. Thanks to his mediation, more than half a million prisoners-of-war were able to return to their own countries from the camps in Central Europe and Russia, and he saved millions of people from starvation in the Volga regions and the Ukraine. His name is also connected with the passports which allowed stateless persons to build up a new existence after the war.

The 'Fram' also reminds us of Nansen's great successor, Roald Amundsen, whose mother-ship she was on his expedition to the South Pole. With the conquest of the Antarctic in 1911, the classic period of polar exploration on the ice came to an end, and the aeroplane and the airship took over. Amundsen also made several attempts to reach the North Pole by air. He lost his life in a crash over the Arctic Ocean while he was trying to bring help to his Italian colleague, General Nobile, whose airship had got into difficulties.

Not far from 'Fram House', in a more modern building, Thor Heyerdahl's famous raft, the Kon-Tiki, is on exhibition. Heyerdahl sailed across the Pacific Ocean in a hundred days on this primitive balsa-wood construction—bound together in Indian fashion—in order to prove his theory that the South Sea Islands had originally been populated from South America.

In the immediate vicinity of these famous vessels of our own day, there are what may well be described as Norway's greatest attraction—two old Viking ships, which prove to what extent sea-faring is a Norwegian heritage. Fifty years ago the sensational find of these two well-preserved Viking ships, which had lain for a thousand years in the mud at the bottom of the outermost part of Oslo Fjord, delighted the hearts of archaeologists. One of these vessels was a magnificently carved luxury ship, sumptuously decorated, which still contained the mortal remains of a pagan queen and the jewellery that had been buried with her. The other ship was of the Gogstad type, one of those fast slender vessels used by the Vikings on their long voyages to distant lands. The Vikings journeyed on board these sailing-ships to Iceland, Greenland, and the mythical Vinland, as they called America. Proof is believed to exist that one of these vessels made four journeys to Vinland 500 years before Christopher

Columbus discovered America. The seaworthiness of these ships has been tested, showing just how high the standard of Viking ship-building actually was. An exact copy of a Gogstad ship was sailed across the Atlantic by a crew of thirteen to the World's Fair in Chicago in 1893. The vessel accomplished this journey in forty days at an average speed of 10 knots, showing excellent stability, even in a heavy sea. At the same time, a faithful replica of Columbus's caravel, the 'Santa Maria', was sailed over the same distance, this vessel taking several months to reach its destination.

A country such as Norway, whose coastline of over 3,400 kilometres is the longest in Europe, naturally looks back over an old tradition as a maritime nation. In the age of the sailing-boat, the fleet was scattered about the various small towns along the coast, or lay for the most part in the outer harbours of the innumerable islands off the mainland, while today the merchant fleet is concentrated round the big towns of Oslo, Bergen, Stavanger, Tönsberg, and Sandefjord. Many ships which sail the Seven Seas under the Norwegian flag have never been to their home waters.

Prior to the last World War, the Norwegian merchant fleet amounted to some five million GRT (gross registered tons), or 7% of the total world tonnage. In international shipping, Norway was second only to Great Britain, followed by the U.S.A. and Japan. During the Second World War, the Norwegian fleet was destined to play an undreamed-of rôle in world politics. When Norway was attacked in 1940, one-sixth only of all her ships were stationed in home waters. The entire Norwegian fleet was ordered by the Government to head for the nearest Allied port. Possibly the greatest shipping-company in world history was founded in London and, under the direction of the Norwegian Government in exile, took over a thousand merchant ships, representing a total of four million GRT. During the Battle of London, the Norwegian fleet fulfilled the important task of assuring the petrol supply for the

Royal Air Force bases. The Norwegian ships took over a no less prominent rôle in the Battle of the Atlantic, on convoy duty, and during the Normandy landings. In the words of Noël-Baker, the Norwegian tankers signified as much for their country during the Battle of the Atlantic as the Spitfires did for England during the Battle of Britain, and according to the American General Lands, the Norwegian fleet was worth more to the Allied cause than a million soldiers. But the Norwegian ships were severely affected by the war; one half of the entire tonnage was lost and the remaining units were subjected to tremendous wear and tear. Some 4,500 Norwegian sailors and officers lost their lives in action at sea.

After the war, the rebuilding of the Norwegian merchant fleet became one of the Government's primary tasks; the efforts of the country's shipping-companies were also considerable, a fact illustrated by the increase in shipping from three to fourteen million tons since 1945, when Norway moved up to third place among the merchant fleets of the world. In spite of these impressive figures, the Norwegian share of world-shipping is today no greater than it was before the Second World War; but the Norwegian merchant fleet is, on the whole, more modern than those of other maritime nations and, even quite recently, 10 million out of a total of 18 million gross tons were less than five years old, a significant fact from the point of view of industrial management and commercial policy.

Like all towns that have outgrown their original rural character too rapidly, present-day Oslo also bears in some way the imprint of chance. The situation of the Norwegian capital is unique, but the pattern of the town can hardly be compared with that of other old European cities. The deliberate unpretentiousness of the town reveals nothing of its earlier rustic charm, nor of the pomp of ancient dynasties. But the parks in the centre of the city, and the main street, named after its builder, nevertheless evince the royal touch. With the eye of the military commander, Carl Johan,

Napoleon's ex-general, and King of Norway and Sweden, had the plans drawn up for the castle that was to be built on an elevation on the outskirts of the town, which was then still small. Today, the Norwegian Royal Palace, surrounded by a great park, towers above the capital like a mighty monument, at one end of the magnificent Carl Johan Street. On either side of this imposing thoroughfare lie the old University, built in classical style, and opposite it the National Theatre. As architectural and—perhaps—political counterpoint, the Norwegian Parliament, or Storting, with which the Royal House of Norway and Sweden was often involved in stormy disagreement during the 19th century, is situated near the other end of the street.

On Constitution Day, which is celebrated every year on the 17th of May, when Carl Johan Street resounds with the singing of tens of thousands of Norwegian children marching in procession to the Royal Palace, and when, from the Palace balcony, King and Crown Prince greet the young people of Norway, we are deeply impressed by the buoyancy and zest, and the close feeling of brotherhood among the people of this great, beautiful, and happy country.

Odd Hölaas

29 Lilac in flower near Ullensvang, on Hardanger Fjord
30 Spring in the air on a mountain-lake between Stryn and Geiranger

32

33

34

35

R

7

Norway's Deep-Sea Fishing

The earliest historical records of Norwegian fishing date from the 9th century, the time when the foundations of Norway's legend and literature were laid. Reliable accounts by distinguished contemporary writers tell of great men on the Norwegian coast, who equipped the annual cod and herring-fishing expeditions and marketed the catch in other countries, above all in England. Special interest attaches to the fact that the period of these traditions coincides with the era when the fast slender keel-boats were built, those technically outstanding Viking ships that reached the east coast of North America under Leif Eriksson a full five hundred years before Christopher Columbus. It is, therefore, not surprising that Norwegian fishery was already a highly-developed trade more than a thousand years ago—a trade which understood so well how to exploit the abundance of fish that Nature provided so generously around the country's coasts. Dried fish, walrus-skins for making ships' ropes, and ivory from walrus-tusks were the principal articles of export in those times. The enormous wealth which the old traders discovered on their long journeys was doubtless a source of temptation for the Norwegians of those days, who were still heathens, to resume their piratical activities, as a result of which they went down into history with that reputation for wanton destruction that attaches to the Vikings.

Fishing, however, was a vital source of sustenance for Norway's coastal population long before the regular trade with foreign lands commenced. Archaeological examinations of shore-settlements have produced finds of minute bone fish-hooks, and the left-overs from meals have led to the conclusion that the population lived by the same sort of fishing during the Stone Age, between 2,000 and 5,000 years ago, as that which forms the basis of present-day fishery. The bones of fish which live exclusively at greater depths prove that, during the Stone Age, the Norwegians already possessed boats which enabled them to go far out beyond the sheltered coastal waters.

Until the turn of the century, Norwegian fishing largely retained the character of coastal-fishery, owing to the country's geographical situation. Off the coast, the Continental Shelf forms a belt of shallow water several hundred kilometres wide, which stretches to where the Continental Slope reaches depths of 3,000 to 4,000 metres (c. 10,000–13,000 ft). The Norwegian fishermen also call this belt of water the 'Waders' Sea'; it is the breeding and spawning-ground of a teeming abundance of sea-fish. Nature was pleased to bestow a curious shape upon Norway as a country; while measuring 1,725 kilometres (c. 1,080 miles), as the crow flies, from north to south, Norway's coastline, including all the bays and fjords, actually measures 20,000 kilometres (c. 12,500 miles). This coastal formation, protected by the 150,000 islands which lie off the mainland, affords a large number of natural harbours and of regions well suited to cultivation. A significant part of the fishing can, for this reason, be undertaken in inland waters from small boats. At the same time, the harbours serve as convenient points of departure for the open sea, where large-scale deep-sea fishing has developed in recent years.

Since olden times, the backbone of the Norwegian fishing trade has been the great seasonal cod and herring-fishing expeditions. The Norwegian word 'vaer' designates the fishing harbours which serve as starting-points for such expeditions, and the fishermen themselves actually live there. While a harbour of this kind would normally have only a small resident population, it is invaded by thousands of fishermen with their boats at the time of the catch. Here they find shelter from the storms, and the first market for their wares are the merchants who fillet, salt, and dry the fish on the spot, or prepare it for the refrigerating-plants.

The chronicles of the Middle Ages already mention large assemblies of fisher-folk in the harbours, above all those of the Lofoten Islands in northern Norway, and the kings of those days had simple shelters erected for the newcomers. These fishermen's huts were later built by the local inhabitants and let to the fishermen. It is only in more recent times that the old tradition has been lost, for the Norwegian fishing industry is developing rapidly, and the fishing-waters of the modern fleet lie more and more out in the open seas. Even if the seasonal offshore fishing should continue, the fishermen can now live comfortably aboard their own vessels.

For some time, the greatest demand among all the species of fish caught off the Norwegian coast has been for cod and herring. Cod-fishing takes place mostly in the northern coastal waters, particularly along the banks off the Lofoten Islands. The spectacle of the seasonal fishing expedition in full swing off the Lofotens—little short of dramatic—has today attained international fame and has become a leading tourist attraction. Upon the waters below the snow-capped pinnacles of the island mountains, the immense fishing-fleet draws up in lines many kilometres long, veiled in a light haze from the exhaust fumes of its motors. The Lofoten season lasts from the end of January until about Easter, and 30,000 fishermen with 6,000 to 7,000 vessels take part, assembling in the numerous little harbours of the islands.

The migration of the cod from the Barents Sea to the Lofoten Islands and other waters along the Norwegian coast is an extraordinary natural phenomenon. The home of the Arctic-Norwegian cod family, as this species of cod is called, lies between the northernmost part of Norway, Spitsbergen, and Novaya Zemlya off the north coast of Russia. After a period of growth lasting from six to twelve years, when sexual maturity is reached, the cod, called 'skrei' or 'kabeljau' by the Norwegians, sets off on its journey to the Norwegian coast, a distance of many hundreds of kilometres. The 'kabeljau' does not cover this enormous distance merely by chance; water temperatures of between 6° and 7° Centigrade are a requisite condition for spawning. The cod finds this temperature along the Norwegian coast in a shallow layer of water between the cold surface and the warmer and more saline waters of the Gulf Stream at the bottom of the sea.

The Arctic-Norwegian cod is, scientifically speaking, the most thoroughly studied salt-water fish in the world. For over a hundred years, data concerning the size and quality of the fish have been collected. With the help of examinations carried out on the ear-stones of fishes, it has been possible to ascertain their ages, to determine the age of a fish at the time of its first 'honeymoon', and to find out how many times it has visited the Lofotens for the same purpose. If the fish is not caught, it returns once a year to the spawning-ground for twelve to fifteen years. These natives of the Barents Sea swarm southwards in their billions towards the Norwegian coast in an invisible procession, inaudible to the human ear. Neither whale nor bird follows them on their journey, which, far down in the depths, however, is anything but silent. Sensitive listening apparatus, developed during the last war as an anti-submarine device, conveys little hissing sounds to the listener on board the research-ship; these sounds resemble those of a muted conversation and are the manifestation of the constant contact among the fish by means of sound-waves.

Thousands of millions of fertilized eggs are the result of the spawning activity around the Lofotens and the other fishing-banks, a female cod being capable of producing as many as ten million eggs. Only some violent mass-mortality among the young fish can prevent over-population of their native waters, which would inevitably lead to their ultimate extinction. After a preliminary period of growth, lasting a few months, in the vicinity of the coast, the little fish sets off on its journey to the north, often under the protection of a poisonous jelly-fish; here the adolescent fish grows up, to return to Norway later as a full-grown adult cod.

In the course of the last fifty years, cod-fishing has been quantitatively outstripped by herring-fishing in the southern coastal waters between Kristiansund and Haugesund. The migratory habits of the herring, unlike those of the cod, were veiled in mystery until only a few years ago. It was not known whence they came nor which waters

N10BD

38 Skerry-strewn sea off Torghatten
39 Vardö, the most easterly town in Norway
40 Cod hung up to dry at Hammerfest
41 View across the fishing-harbour of Ålesund
42 Up-to-date fish-filleting factory at Hammerfest
43 Modern motor fishing-cutter at Bodö
44 Narvik in the light of the midnight sun
45 Sarpsborg on the Glomma, a wood industry town
46 Whaler in the light of the midnight sun off the coast of Finnmark

41

42

43

44

45

46 ▷

48

49

51

47 Hungry gulls at midnight
48 Future sailors on board a training ship
49 Small dockyard at Ny-Hellesund, near Kristiansand
50 Norwegian tanker at Grimstad, near Kristiansand
51 Richly-carved jib-boom of a training ship in Tromsö harbour
52 In Geiranger Fjord, with the 4795 ft high Geitfonnegga

they chose to go to at the end of the spawning-season. The fact remained that they arrived in vast numbers, though unfortunately at unpredictable intervals. History has shown that the periods of phenomenal herring-fishing off the Norwegian coast last between sixty and seventy years. Thirty to forty years during which hardly a herring is sighted may then elapse between these periods. The last fishing-period, which began at the turn of the century, brought an annually increasing yield, culminating in 1956 with a haul of 1.2 million tons, or 70% of the total Norwegian yield of fish for that year. The following years showed a retrogressive tendency, yet the catch quota of 1962 still amounted to 80,000 tons.

During the favourable fishing-period which has now come to an end, the Norwegian fishing-fleet was considerably enlarged, solely because of the herring-yield. Hundreds of millions of Norwegian crowns were invested in modern shipping units and the processing-plant was also greatly enlarged. The prodigious quantities of herring caught by the Norwegian fishermen could not, of course, be used entirely for human consumption; the larger part of the yield is processed, being made into oil and fish-meal. Owing to the absence of the herring from Norwegian waters today, the fishing-fleet lies largely idle; the winter of 1963/64, however, provided some relief, in that an unexpected and significant herring-catch was made off the Lofoten Islands; the appearance of this fish in the traditional spawning-waters of the cod is a phenomenon hitherto unknown to the present-day generation of fishermen.

From a scientific point of view, this event was, in itself, not surprising. Basing their prognosis on historical documentation, the oceanographers had anticipated both the end of the herring-fishing in south-western Norway and the coincidence in time of the appearance of this fish in the north. With the optimism peculiar to their kind, the deep-sea fishermen refused to believe that the end of the herring-'adventure' had come. A similar situation arose around the middle of the last century, when the herring vanished without any warning after having put in a regular appearance over a long period. A hundred years ago, this abrupt discontinuation of the herring-fishing led to a serious economic depression along the coast, which was accompanied by all the symptoms of a disastrous crisis. Today the situation is different, as adequate reserves have been laid down in the course of the good fishing years, and the fleet has been equipped with large ocean-going vessels suitable for action in distant waters.

The Norwegian fishing-trade does not, of course, confine itself to catching these two species of fish. Large quantities of the local coastal cod—as opposed to the Barents Sea cod—the green cod, otherwise known as coalfish or rock salmon, halibut, flounder, mackerel, as well as dogfish, shrimps, prawns, crabs, lobster, and salmon, are also caught. The small salmon native to the Barents Sea is a speciality which, although unsuitable for human consumption, in good years forms the basis of an abundant oil and fish-meal production.

The more limited the coastal fishery becomes, the greater is the interest shown by the fishermen in the distant fishing-grounds. Deep-sea fishing takes place mainly in the waters off Greenland, Björnöya, Spitsbergen, the Shetland Isles, the Faroe Islands, Iceland, and Newfoundland; a local herring is also caught in the North Sea.

The political discussion in Parliament have not been without a certain influence on the development of the modern Norwegian fishing-trade. Until present times the fisher-folk—above all those of the northern regions—have divided their labours between the seasonal fishing and agriculture on a modest scale. They regarded the intervention of the Government in fishery matters as a threat to the fisherman's traditional right to equip and own his boat. The opposition of the fishermen to the modern equipment of the coastal fishing-fleet, above all with drag-nets, was obstinate and tedious. Obstructionism on the part of the workers with regard to an industry is, in similar circumstances, a well-known phenomenon, also in other countries. Finally, however, in spite of the weighty objections, it was possible to create a highly efficient, if not very large, drag-net fleet for the purpose of assuring adequate supplies of raw materials for the fish-processing plant constructed with State aid in northern Norwegian towns. One of the most important of these plants was set up in the town of Hammerfest, in the extreme north of the country, by the Nestlé concern and, like all other refrigeration-plants, is dependent on an uninterrupted supply of fish throughout the year.

The Government, the competent fishing-trade authorities, and the oceanographers are today devoting themselves more and more to the question of the dwindling numbers of the fish which have afforded so many branches of industry a lucrative livelihood for many hundreds of years.

This applies principally to the Arctic-Norwegian cod, the yield of which has, during recent years, shown a disturbing retrograde tendency off the Lofoten Islands. While hauls of up to 145,000 tons were recorded during the years following the Second World War and 80,000 tons, which represents a satisfactory catch, could be regularly counted on, the yield sank from year to year until it finally amounted to no more than 30,000 to 40,000 tons. Sea-fishing was, of course, always subject to fluctuations, which were also clearly evident in the case of the cod; but investigations into the quantities of fish have revealed an unmistakable decimation precisely in the case of the Arctic-Norwegian branch of the cod family and particularly in the Barents Sea, where the drag-nets of many countries take a high toll of the cod-shoals, the half-grown fish also falling prey to the nets. While, until recently, it was exclusively the Norwegians who engaged in cod-fishing in these northernmost waters, their share accounts for only around 25% of the total catch today.

Endeavours to increase the size of the drag-net mesh in order to protect the young fish have been made on an international basis, but so far this reform has been put into effect only by the Norwegians, to set a good example to their rivals.

To what extent the concentrated exploitation has affected the various species of herring is a moot point. Of this fish we know that it appears periodically at particularly lengthy intervals and that it is in greater demand on the market than it used to be. Norway's main competitor in herring-fishing is the Soviet Union, which follows the fish-shoals on the high seas with extensive fishing-fleets, exploiting the yield on the spot aboard large industrial vessels. In this connection, mention should be made of Norwegian oceanography, which maintains its own State-controlled Institute in Bergen. The high scientific standard of this establishment enjoys international prestige, and such names as G. O. Sars, Fridtjof Nansen, Johan Hjort, and Harald Sverdrup are connected with it. The last-mentioned was at one time a director of the great oceanographical centre at La Jolla in California.

With his scientific study of the cod family, Gunnar Rollefsen, Director of the Oceanographical Institute, has played an outstanding rôle in recent years. Finn Devold has devoted himself to research on the herring, and he has succeeded in determining the movements of the herring-shoals. The herring proved to be a migratory fish, which covered thousands of kilometres annually on its journeys to and from the spawning-grounds. However, it has not yet been possible to predict with sufficient precision when it will re-visit the Norwegian coast and when it will leave it again.

In the international sphere, Norwegian oceanography has held the lead for many years, even if it has been overtaken today in some branches as the result of the growing interest of other great nations in deep-sea fishing. It is hoped, by means of rational exploitation, to open up enormous additional sources of sea-fish in order to supply the growing food requirements of the world's rapidly increasing population. The consistently high level of Norwegian oceanography has taken on more and more significance in this connection. The Institute in Bergen has a staff of outstanding scientific specialists, and its two research-ships, both built for service on the high seas, are among the best equipped in the world.

The decline in the total Norwegian fish-yield, which becomes more apparent each year, indicates clearly the decrease in the numbers of the fish in northern waters. In the years following 1950, the average annual Norwegian fish-yield amounted to as much as two million tons, while the figure later sank to somewhat more than one million tons. From 1960 to 1969, the total Norwegian fish-yield amounted again (1967 more than 3 million tons, 1969 2.2 million tons).

Until recently, Norway was third among all the great fishing nations of the world; today she is fifth after Peru, Japan, the Soviet Union, and China. During the last ten years, the total world fish-yield has increased from 38 to 64 million tons, and countries such as Japan and the Soviet Union today fish in all the Seven Seas.

With a population of 3.8 million, Norway has retained its lead among all the world's fishing-nations as far as its *per capita* yield is concerned, and Norway's export of fish-products is unequalled by any other country. The number of Norwegian fishermen actively engaged in fishing has decreased considerably during recent years, because the use of large ships and highly efficient navigational and fishing equipment has brought in its wake a reduction of the man-power required. Of today's 60,000 fishermen, 23,000 are engaged exclusively in the fishing-trade, while the remainder combine fishing with an occupation on the mainland. Thousands of fisher-folk still take part in agriculture, fishing only on a seasonal basis. Not infrequently they will run a modest fishing-trade, catching their fish in the nearby inland waters to supply their own requirements or those of their immediate neighbours.

To what extent Norway is able to prepare its fish-yield for export is illustrated by statistics, according to which 15% of the total amount of fish caught is sold on the home market. Data concerning the number and sizes of the Norwegian fishing-vessels also throw interesting light on the character of this specifically national trade. The fishing-fleet comprises some 36,000 ships, with a total displacement of 390,000 tons; of these vessels only 9,000 are covered motor-boats, the majority being open, even though, without exception, motor-driven units.

Fishing is a hard and exacting occupation. It is practised in exceedingly rough and storm-swept waters and entails a great variety of difficulties, especially in winter, when the polar night is penetrated by only a pale shimmer of light for a few hours each day. Many tragedies occur during the winter hurricanes and shipwrecks frequently cause loss of human life. But the wealth of fish which lie beneath the storm-tossed surface of the ocean will never cease to cast its spell upon mankind. As long as the mighty foam-capped waves of the Atlantic Ocean continue to break against the cliffs of Norway's cleft coastline, the inhabitants of that country, sheltering behind the wind-swept islands off the mainland, will not cease to set out and re-live, year after year, the fascinating adventure of deep-sea fishing.

Asbjörn Barlaup

53 Polar alpine landscape between Sogne Fjord and Gudbrandsdal
54 Tongue of the Briksdalbree glacier
55 Narrow gorge above Fortun i Luster
56 The 525 ft high waterfall of the Skjeggedalsfoss at Hardanger
57 M.S. *Oslofjord* of the Norske-Amerika-Linje bound for Maråk
58 Sunk in contemplation of the Svartis massif
59 On the shores of Lake Tyn, in Jotunheim 3536 ft above sea-level
60 A landscape, almost Arctic in character, on the Gorsvatn, between Bergen and Oslo
61 'Ocean Viking', Norwegian oil and gaz drilling station above 'Ekofisk' deposit in the North Sea
62/63 On a trip to northern Norway, north of Trondheim
64 Tromsö harbour
65 The bridge, 5050 ft in length, joining Tromsö with the mainland
66 Wooden loading-ramp and old steamship plying locally in Sogne Fjord
67 Modern ferry-boat between Narvik and Fauske
68 View of the huge Svartis glacier from Oernes
69 Beacon in the dangerous outer skerries of Hammerfest

54

55

56

57

59

60

62

63

64▷

N8080

KVALSUND
TROMSØ

SELTRYKK
X 4 TONN

66

◁65

67

Norway and World Shipping

In accordance with the request of the Norwegian author, style and character of the following contributions have been left largely unchanged in the English version

Consider the map of the world—is it possible to see at a glance which are the shipping countries? Why do Belgium and Finland have small merchant navies? Is it possible to see from the map that Denmark, Norway, and Sweden together, with a population of a mere 15 million and no Commonwealth to serve, have aggregated a fleet larger than that of Great Britain, the World's Number One? [The United States are excepted, since many of their ships are mothballed.] Why has Norway the second-largest operating fleet in the world, with about 18 million gross tons? Why has she twice as much tonnage as Denmark's and Sweden's together, and why has it been increasing every year at twice the rate of Denmark's and Sweden's together, and even faster in the last few years? How is the fact to be explained that, with a population of just over one-third that of London, Norway has ten times as many tons *per capita* as Great Britain? Oslo, Norway's small capital, has 7 million tons, almost 30% of Great Britain's fleet. And why is Scandinavia building one-and-a-half million gross tons of ships, second only to Japan?

The sea is fraught with danger for Man, who is born ashore. In a flat, tillable, not over-populated country with a temperate climate, Man will stay where he is. If the land is not too rocky, roads can be built even with archaic tools, and the innate cheapness of sea-borne transportation per ton-mile will remain unknown.

People who live behind a short coastline, open to swells and tides and changing shoals will not learn to swim, to row, or to sail small craft. There will be no natural boyhood training for seamanship. There will be big boats, or none at all; for frequently the passage in and out of artificial harbours is very dangerous. Breakwaters have cost the life of many a ship.

If Norway is swung round on the pivot of her southernmost headland, her northernmost cape will almost touch North Africa. The country is partly Arctic and preponderantly mountainous. Owing to the altitude of these mountains, the character of Norway is in many places tantamount to 'Arctic', even in the south. It is tempting, therefore, to deduce that Norway must be primitive. This would be true if she supported 50 million people instead of her 3.8 million, and if her area were that of Britain or Italy.

Admittedly, only about 4% of Norway is tillable, and 27% in all, including the forests, is suitable for plant life. However, while over-population may result in poor nations in rich areas, the opposite is also true. Despite the small agricultural area available, the Norwegians' *per capita* 'ration' is by no means small. The nation could withstand a blockade by simply changing its diet and taking certain other measures. For each Italian or Briton to have an equal agricultural ration, 50% of Italy or Great Britain would have to be tillable, and 400% would have to be suitable for plants. Norway has a modern standard of living today, as well as the advantage, rare today, of being able to enjoy the unspoilt nature of her forests and mountains as a free park available to all. Norway is warmed by the Gulf Stream, and is climatically entirely different from the western Atlantic parallels. Only the tropical midday sun is always higher than Norway's in her summer season. And while the tropical sun shines for twelve hours, Norway's midsummer sun works up to twenty-four hours a day—and plants grow as long as the sun shines. Limpid air means better sun penetration; wheat will ripen in the same number of days in the south of Norway as in the south of France. Oslo has July temperatures similar to those of London or Paris, and grapes and peaches may be grown. Arctic lakes may be tepid in summer and, warmed by the Midnight Sun, ocean bays often reach 20° C. The inner Oslo Fjord in July is as warm as Channel resorts in August. With practically no tides, the sun-warmed sea-water remains in the fjord.

In other words, the main problem of Norway's inhabitants is not climatic, and only partly geographic. It is mainly topographical and geological. Rockless countries built roads with spades and wheelbarrows until better equipment speeded up the process; but there was no process to speed up in Norway. Before the advent of explosives and motorized equipment, roads were mostly technically impossible. Modern equipment improved the roads in other countries; Norway, however, was *changed* by them. She was born.

From the outset, Norway's predicament has been one of transportation; even today, 80% of her people live less than 20 km. from the coast. But explosives and road-making equipment have brought her into line with other nations. She is poor no longer.

It was no Viking who coined the phrase that sea transport is by far the cheapest per ton-mile. They could sail across a fjord ten times faster than they could make their way round it among trees, rocks, and brambles. They could sail to distant towns in a few days—walking or riding would have taken as many weeks.

With the exception of a few stretches, Norway is screened from the fierce sea by an intricate system of fjords penetrating up to 200 km. inland, and by a fantastic assortment of isles and skerries, behind which even small craft are relatively snug. Here there is fish in plenty and side by side with the commercial fisheries there is also the economically important daily household fishing for a free dinner. The waters are pleasant for bathing and boating. There are eggs, berries, and pasture-land on the islands. As the farmer was 'born on skis' (*ski* in Norwegian = strip of wood), so the coastal lad was born in a boat. There was wood in profusion. Water-borne traffic was used where other transportation could not exist. The Viking ships were evolved, and ventured out beyond the Skerry Guard.

The poor Norsemen craved the enviable riches of the 'developed' countries of those days. With nothing much to sell, and with 'unilateral' trade piling deficits in the ledgers, they settled accounts by exterminating their suppliers. They invaded England. They rolled their ships overland far into France, and, sailing up the Seine, made an unsuccessful attack on Paris, and finally they settled in the region of present-day Normandy.

They colonized Iceland, Greenland, and the Faroes. They discovered North America in 1000 A.D. William the Conqueror's victory at the Battle of Hastings in 1066 may have been due partly to the fact that the English were still exhausted after their own victory a few days earlier at Stamford Bridge, where the Norsemen lost an appalling number of their men. Norway's period of gruesome piracy eventually came to an end. She built up her trade with many countries after she had sunk from being a leading military power into virtual oblivion for centuries. Around 1350, the Black Death wiped out one-fourth of Europe's population, and in Norway vast areas reverted to uninhabited wilderness. Norway was united with Denmark, becoming virtually a colony. Her language was influenced by Danish, and books and music were printed for the most part in Copenhagen. While the countries further south were able to build splendid ships and could afford luxuries, rocky Norway suffered poverty and want.

The later Vikings caught various small species of whale; and in Normandy, it seems, they taught the Basques, who in their turn were the first to evolve a method of harpooning the medium-sized 'right' whales in the Bay of Biscay, and even ventured out into the Atlantic, together with the Portuguese.

In 1596 the Dutchman, Willem Barents, vainly seeking a short-cut to China for its tea by the north-east passage, had discovered Spitsbergen. At the same time, however, he observed enormous schools of 'right' whales and also the huge fast-moving 'finner' species of whale, which had until then not been within the reach of the hunters. The fact that Holland became the second nation to commence whaling north of

Arctic Norway is due to this Willem Barents, who died at Novaya Zemlya. The British started in 1612, the Dutch close at their heels, both having learnt from the Spaniards. The ensuing competition ended with a division of the fishing-grounds—the best for the British, whose Navy was the strongest, followed by the Dutch, while the Spaniards were allotted what was left over.

The British whalers had flat rates of pay and hunted less energetically than the Dutch, who received a percentage—a system of payment still in force. In summer, the Dutch had about 16,000 men taking part in whaling activities up in the north, including the boiling-station in Norway. This immense slaughter of whales was remunerative for a century, but by then the number of the mammals was greatly reduced, and the hunt was transferred to Greenland. It should be noted, however, that it was the Dutch who discovered this source of wealth, while the Norwegians passively allowed a century of multi-national whaling practically on their doorstep. King Christian IV of Denmark and Norway, however, dispatched men-of-war up to the north in an unsuccessful attempt to exact duties. How was this possible? Southern Norse shipping had arisen as a result of poverty, and whaling was fraught with such financial risks that it could be practised only by communities already rich enough to face possible failure. Norway's extreme north possessed rowing-boats, fish, and game, but no leeway for the next winter's pinch.

Holland amassed great wealth from her North Sea fisheries, built excellent ships, and expanded over the world. The Dutch founded Cape Town and New Amsterdam, later re-named New York, and they had surpassed the British at whaling. Some time after moving west, however, the Dutch were faced with grave problems at home, and the British overtook them in whaling. The whaling-grounds were now close to New England, whose hard-working, temperate Puritans soon founded a hegemony. Actually, this hegemony was infinitely greater than Europeans seem to realise. European whaling was gradually subsidized, or was carried out with either American men, American equipment, American ships, or American owners—or all four together.

Holland was obliged to watch Britain gradually spreading her Empire over the world. Continental Holland had frontiers. Just as it was not the Vikings, so it was not the insular British, who coined the phrase about sea-transport being cheaper per ton-mile. The British just throve, water-borne. Heavy cannon could not be dragged overland, small cannon only with difficulty. The British Navy could smash up La Rochelle, and then sail on and do the same at La Pallice.

Sea-transport won the wars in 1918 and 1945. Inland minds had never fully appreciated this, in spite of the fact that they had seen 500-ton barges being hauled by two men on the canal tow-paths, and though they were fully aware that it would require a hundred lorries, engines, and drivers if road-transport were employed.

Fulton's s/s *Clermont,* the first steamer, ploughed the Hudson as far back as 1807, but steamboats still did not constitute a threat to sailing vessels. In bays and fjords, the Norwegians still built and derived profits from small wooden boats for fishing and coastal traffic. In subsequent winters, with these profits, they built larger vessels and sailed to France with timber and planks, or blocks of ice, and returned with grain. If no cargo could be found in that country, they sought it elsewhere, and having acquired a reputation for arriving safely and handling the cargoes with care, they were entrusted with wares to and from still more countries.

Shipwrights, skippers, forest owners, and others pooled their resources to own a ship. They relied on good ships and first-rate crews, who had almost been born in boats. Boys born in the coastal regions had to drag the baker's cart in poverty—or go to sea. This, too, was badly paid, but at least it spelt romance and adventure. In many merchant navies one could rise from the position of officer's apprentice to that of captain, or maybe from cabin-boy to bos'n. Norwegian captains had nearly all once been cabin-boys; there was no 'afore and abaft-the-mast' tradition. They were one. This was democracy. Workers ashore could not switch to administration and advance in the same way.

The British Navigation Act crippled world trade for centuries. 'Cargo for Britain in British bottoms' went so far that East Indian coffee taken to Amsterdam on a Dutch ship could not be sold to London without deviating, for instance, to Cape Town first, in order to travel British to London. Abolition of the Act was vociferously advocated, but in the House of Lords, Lord Moffat held that this would drive Britain from the high seas, unless she employed Norwegians and Lascars. The Norwegians built good ships at half the British price, and put up with black bread and one-third of the British meat ration. The Act was finally abolished in 1849, and resulted in a new departure in world trade and shipping.

The Navigation Act had provided that Britain's ships must be home-built, which was unobjectionable if they were the best. An owner in global competition, however, must be free to acquire his vessel wherever he can procure her best and cheapest, because international shipping ignores all frontiers and wage discrepancies. New England was now building those incredibly graceful clippers, the fastest and cheapest vessels in the world, with up-to-date equipment on board—and there were Maury's superior sailing routes. By 1860, after the abolition of the Navigation Act, the U.S. merchant fleet was somewhat smaller than that of the British Empire, but in consequence of more rapid reshipment, America led in international transportation by sea. Meanwhile, U.S. whaling had also been enjoying a profitable hegemony, while that of other countries had to be subsidized. Around 1840, North America had 735 whaling ships, Britain only 14.

Then great changes took place. While British ship-owners were now allowed to purchase ships wherever they liked, a new law ruled that American ships must be American-built. When metal and steam entered the arena, Britain recaptured her lead in ship-construction. It was now the American owners' turn to be handicapped, and this law is still in force.

Oil was discovered in America, and there was a general belief that petroleum would soon push whale-oil lamps off the market. Attempts were made to construct ocean-going ships for the transport of oil in bulk instead of in casks and cans. It would have been natural for optimistic, far-sighted, efficient America to develop these vessels. It would also have been obvious for the Americans to adopt modern methods of whaling and processing, particularly as the species that could be caught with hand-harpoons from rowing-boats were rapidly being exterminated. During all these centuries, the huge fin-whale, or rorqual, had not only been left untouched, they had also been multiplying and thriving on the additional food that resulted from the decimation of the medium-sized species, such as the 'right' whales.

Some Americans did experiment, however, though half-heartedly and expensively, and failed. America withdrew from whaling and, a few years later, also from competitive shipping. There has been no come-back in either field so far.

After much pioneering, the New World was paying good dividends, and east-coast America ventured upon the lucrative 'Winning of the West', which sucked enterprise inland. America was no longer a cheap country—a Boston crossing-sweeper earned as much as three whalers. It was the same with the merchantmen. Rich America priced herself off the waves. The void was filled chiefly by Britain and Norway. Rich nations were substituting steel steamboats for wooden sailing ships, but paradoxically much of the coal for the developing bunkering-stations was carried in sailing vessels. Norway had no capital other than seamanship and sweat, 'know-how' and savings. She acquired as many as she could of the world's superannuated windjammers, otherwise destined for scrapping.

With these second-hand vessels, Norway rose to shipping nation number 3: with 1½ million gross tons, and some 50,000 sailors. Much Chauvinistic poetry and national romance was inspired by this canvas glory—ragged glory. Sometimes a ship had to have belly-chains to hold it together! 'Is this seamanship?', it was asked. It certainly was. Anyone could sail safely with brand-new, expensive ships bought by wealth ashore. Seamanship consisted in taming these 'coffins', on poor provisions and low pay, yet arrive safely and even improve the reputation for service—and acquire into the bargain more and brand-new ships from the hard-earned money gained aboard these very old ones.

Gradually, the Norwegians had more tonnage than their own local traffic needed, and more and more they began to ply exclusively between foreign countries. Once 200 Norwegian vessels could be seen in the timber-port of Pensacola at the same time, and on another occasion 10,000 Norwegian seamen celebrated New Year's Eve in New York. The Norwegians were everywhere, dominating the American freight market. They sailed the Seven Seas, found ports, cargoes, trade, new possibilities, while their homeland had next to nothing to offer them.

Throughout much of the 19th century, Norway had a high birth-rate and wholesale emigration took place. If three generations are taken into account—children, parents, and grandparents—there are today more 'Norwegians' in America than in Norway itself. In addition to the 50,000 sailing in Norwegian ships, they also helped to man American vessels to such an extent that, in many of them, Americans and other nationals learnt Norwegian, 'the ship's lingo'.

Hesitatingly, Norway, too, adopted steam and steel. But her late canvas boom had put her back in steamship construction. Such vessels cost more, and so the tonnage dwindled. The steam-engine was a British invention. Britain had coal, and had initiated the Industrial Revolution. The Empire had reached its zenith. A colossal fleet carried manufactured goods out, raw materials home, passengers both ways. Serving national purposes, this fleet was assured freight, and British yards built the best ships. Other nations, fearing dependence upon Great Britain's merchantmen, felt that they must run their own as a national insurance. Some reserved coastal shipping for their national flag. Others ran heavily subsidized national 'prestige fleets'. Flag discrimination became a fact.

However, even the formidable British fleet was insufficient for British purposes. A great many ships were chartered from Norway, who was also Britain's best shipyard customer—as many as five out of six ships being built by any yard might be for Norwegian owners. Further British expansion would have alarmed the world even more. Many British owners already had more shipping and other activities than they could staff and handle. Many a trustworthy Norwegian captain or shipping man was therefore offered means to start on his own. This helped Norway and eased international tension. Norway's fleet belonged to no threatening Super Power. Navigating in the shade of the Great Powers' mutual jealousy, these ships could be chartered by anyone, serving as a lightning-conductor and a joint world reserve.

Shortly after the discovery of petroleum, attempts were made to construct tankers, and the first one was loaded in New York in 1870. They were not technically or commercially good enough. From 1878 to 1886, in Norway's 1,000-year-old town of Tönsberg, Captain Even Tollefsen designed and built six economically and technically sound ocean tankers for carrying bulk petroleum from America to Europe. Tollefsen—to whom Tönsberg has erected a monument—achieved what America had left undone because she had concentrated her energies upon opening up the West. Slightly earlier, Captain Svend Foyn, another Tönsberg man, had developed modern industrial whaling.

The transition from wood and canvas to steam and steel in shipping was mechanization merely for higher efficiency, and there is a widespread belief that, in the same way, modern industrial whaling only implied adding James Watt to orthodox whaling, and that someone would have done it if Foyn had not. This is a mistaken notion. First, the whales were not the same. After centuries of overkilling, 'right' whales and other species of intermediate size that are easily caught were dying out, and the world thought that whaling was nearing its end. Because some small species of whale were becoming scarce, people stated that whaling was finished, while in truth species that attained a length of thirty metres were thriving as never before, because nobody had been able to touch them. And this was what Svend Foyn set out to do.

A 'right' whale could be harpooned by hand and might race about towing the rowing-boat for a long time before it tired and died, and then its thick layer of blubber would make it remain afloat. On the other hand, the blue whale, the biggest of the 'finner' whales, weighed as much as 25 elephants or 150 oxen. Its 7-metre babies gained over 200 pounds daily on their mother's milk. On one occasion a harpooned blue whale tore loose after having towed four rowing-boats, six lines, and the barque for fourteen hours.

These whales had to be killed—no problem in itself, because naval guns could do this—but not from rowing-boats. Moreover, in contrast to the 'right' whales, these creatures had a thin layer of blubber and their carcases sank to the bottom. They would therefore have to be harpooned from some kind of steam-propelled catcher, and simultaneously killed by an explosive shell, preferably from the same cannon in one shot, unimpeded by harpoon cordage, which would, however, have to be strong enough to hold when the carcase was steam-winched from the sea-bottom afterwards and inflated to remain afloat.

This looked technically, financially, and commercially unfeasible. American attempts had failed economically and technically. Svend Foyn's venture would have been utterly useless had not capitalist, inventor, skipper, and business manager been one and the same, a man of strength and determination. He went sealing in the spring, returned with his catch, and set out north on the proceeds. Eventually he invested well over £ 10,000 of his sealing proceeds in his experiments. He developed a fivefold invention, the outstanding features of which were the steam whale-catcher and the single cannon with the explosive shell-nosed harpoon. For the first time, after centuries of whaling, Man conquered the huge creatures.

In 1904, after Foyn, and later also two dozen of his competitors, had practically emptied those waters, whaling was prohibited by the Storting in Norwegian territorial waters off the north coast. Throughout those 35 years, the whole process had been perfected, including the preparation of oil, meat, and other products. Old-fashioned foreign whaling lingered on until 1906, as if Foyn-whaling had not existed. Since the world ignored modern industrial whaling, it remained an almost unchallenged Norwegian monopoly for decades.

This is explained by the fact that Europe's whaling had mostly been either subsidized or American-controlled; and as America priced herself off the sea, and the world's only genuine whaling community vanished, a complete void ensued. The whaling spirit was reborn in Norway's tiniest county, Vestfold, where sociological and other factors were favourable. Although modern whaling was carried on from other parts of Norway, Vestfold, with the towns of Tönsberg and Larvik, became the centre, Sandefjord gradually the Mecca of international whaling. There were practically no potential imitators in other countries.

Already before 1904, Christian Christensen of Sandefjord had experimented on substituting a factory-ship for the shore station. When whaling in Norwegian territorial waters was stopped by law, the industry had to go out of business or move elsewhere. Some steered into the Atlantic. In 1905, Christensen directed his 'floating factory' *Admiralen* to try the Antarctic, using South Georgia as a base. Already the year before, after securing capital in Buenos Aires, Captain C. A. Larsen had commenced this very thing in a venture in which everything was Norwegian except the shareholders and the flag; but it has remained a thorn in the Norwegian flesh to this day that another flag was the first in the Antarctic—though Captain Larsen is not to blame for this. As usual, it had been impossible to raise enough capital in Norway.

Some land stations in South Georgia and elsewhere in the Falkland area, and a good many floating factories, were granted British concessions. The factory-ships also had to have bases for coaling and water supplies. Later, whaling was attempted around Africa and South America, and more or less everywhere else in the world. Moreover, other nations had now come on the scene. Until 1925, flensing took place alongside the floating factories, on adapted passenger or cargo ships; then a Norwegian company introduced a slipway for hauling, flensing, and dismembering the carcases on deck. A few years later, the first specially-constructed factory-ship was designed by a Norwegian and built in Ireland. Independent of shore bases, whaling turned wholly pelagic—and was back to the old-time Iberian approach.

Gradually, whaling had become international. It was stopped by World War II, but was later resumed. During those years, Norway had up to 60% of the world tonnage, but a much larger share of the whaling craft, for while non-Norwegian expeditions had their own crews and specialists, they mostly used Norwegian gunners and other professional whalers.

However, the huge fin-whales also became fewer; and as Japan needed both oil and meat, had lower running expenses and became highly efficient, she bought both British and Norwegian ventures and whale quotas—and in the early 1960's, took over Norway's position as whaling nation number 1. A century ago, North America's wealth had priced her out of her whaling and shipping hegemonies. Now, Norway priced her whaling hegemony over to Japan. But well before her whaling saga had come to an end, the tiny Vestfold county, with 175,000 inhabitants, had gradually turned to her other local invention, the tanker, as well as to general shipping and industries ashore. Today, Vestfold has a merchant fleet of over two million gross tons, which is largely explained by her 100-year whaling interlude.

As the battered second-hand wooden sailing-ships had gradually gone out of service, and steamers had taken their place, so the Norwegian merchant navy had shrunk. But Norway picked up, ordered special trade designs, started cargo lines. Practically all tankers were the property of admiralties or oil companies. There was no independent tanker-market to speak of and, being used to tramp shipping, most owners were afraid of this single-purpose ship. Well before the outbreak of World War I, however, independent Norwegians had also ordered tankers. It was typical that, around 1912, an owner in Tönsberg, the virtual birth-place of the tanker, acquired five 12,000-ton tankers, which were going to do very well indeed.

By 1914, with her 20 million tons, Britain had almost half the world fleet. Norway with 2½ million tons ranked fourth. Though neutral in World War I, Norway sailed for the Western Allies and was badly strafed, losing 51% of her tonnage, more than any of the belligerents. She also lost 2,000 men.

Norway made a great deal of money during the war, but she squandered it in a spirit of immaturity, though it was also partly because Political Economy had not been developed in Norway at the time. Her currency slumped, and she had to pass through many hard years. But eventually the fleet was rebuilt, creeping up to, then passing, the pre-war tonnage figure, by endeavouring to live up to the classic slogan 'build cheap in a slump, run in a boom, tighten the belt and plough back profits for expansion and a better fleet.' The world was rapidly becoming motorized and was clamouring for rivers of oil and oil-derivates. The large oil companies were compelled to expand their wells and refineries; they needed tanks, petrol stations, research, and ships. But they could not cope with everything.

In 1926, The Anglo-Saxon Oil Company offered for international sale, on 80% credit, thirty-seven of her steam-tankers, with ten-year charters to herself. The conditions were generally deemed to leave too slender a margin of profit, so the world did not rise to the bait. The bulk of the ships were bought by Norwegians—mostly newcomers, not existing owners. As it turned out, they averaged £ 12,500 profit per annum before depreciation and interest, a success which helped to consolidate Norway's reputation in this field. The tanker-market was now in Norway, as it were, since both British and American oil companies approached Norwegian owners direct whenever they wanted more charter tonnage. If each oil company had owned sufficient tankers for their peak traffic, there would have been too many. So they left it to the Norwegians to supply a joint reserve, a rôle Norwegian general shipping had been playing for a long time.

Norway, as always, lacked capital. However, an unusual idea for obtaining credit was conceived. An impecunious but knowledgeable and enterprising Norwegian shipping clerk signed a 10-year Oil Company Charter covering depreciation, dividends, salaries, and expenses. On the strength of this safe contract and for very little in cash, a yard built him a ship to be paid for in the same annual instalments as the oil company freights. The clerk became a ship-owner. Ten years later, the ship was written off, whether it was fit only for the scrapyard or not, and so became his unencumbered property. Fortunately, very few in the shipping line outside Norway could believe in this system. Moreover, many people did not consider that a tanker was a ship. Even

70 View from Stalheimskleiv into the Naerödal
71 In the skerry-strewn sea between Lillesand and Kristiansand
72 The Varanger Peninsula, seen from the northern stronghold of Vardöhus
73 The mouth of the Tista, seen from the southern stronghold of Fredriksten
74 On Lofoten Island, off the north-west coast of Norway
75 Lofoten: lowering sky over the skerries

the man in the street believed that petrol was dangerously corrosive to steel. Discharged petrol tankers had been seen knee-deep in rust. Shipping periodicals published panicky articles on rust and corrosion, asking what would happen if the tanker fell apart after only eight years, with two instalments still owing and no freight coming in? Headline 'Norwegian Lunatic Asylum'.

This story kept competition away and thus the conditions remained favourable for the Norwegians. Norway had been running her tankers since the 'seventies. Callipers proved that the plates were not endangered. Petrol contained acid, it was true, but aluminium blocks placed in the holds could and did electro-plate and protect the interior. If this was also labelled 'Nautical Poker', though based on sound figures, the corrosion scare was less important than habitual thinking, which clashed with the idea of 'high-geared finance *cum* pre-construction charter'. Industries ashore turned out their products, hoping to sell them at a profit. They took this for granted, and would have been shocked if told it was a gamble. A liner shipping-company gambled on obtaining cargoes and remunerative freights. They knew that this was so, for they preferred high stock and low bonded capital—and a smaller fleet.

Shares and bonds alike are debts in the company ledgers and merely different forms of investment; however, people are apt to regard bonds as a debt, but not so shares. If borrowers should keep 'dangerous' bonds low, lenders will also register the danger. If a New York bank loans 50% to a Lapland ceramics-works and it fails: what can the bank do? Norwegian shipping had been allowed as much as 105% credit, for the prospective owner had to live while his ship was being built. Why was this not hazardous? Because the New York bank could not move the ceramics-works from Lapland and run it, but the oil company could take over the ship by signing some papers, include it in its own fleet and order it anywhere. As a matter of fact, the collateral was worth a hundred per cent.

72

◁ 71

73

74

75

76

76 Southern point of Jomfruland Island, north of Kragerö Fjord
77 The Saltström connects Skjerstad Fjord with the open sea
78 Tussock-grasses make the Saltström difficult of access
79 On Lofoten Island

The shipowner could shoulder the debt because he himself did not gamble on employment or freight rates, and the high bond percentage proved the opposite of recklessness. The oil company assured itself tonnage: at a lower rate than trip-charter averages. They co-operated, each party handling its own speciality. Instead of investing 100% and operating expensively, the oil company relieved itself of 10% of the capital burden, ensured the owner's self-interest, and let him operate at cheaper rates for them both. The Norwegians obtained this business because they did not consider it madness or witchcraft. They obtained practically all of it, because habitual, hidebound thinking prevented others from competing—and Norway acquired the world's largest fleet of independent tankers and a virtually unchallenged monopoly.

There was a general increase in Norway's mercantile marine, due not to tankers alone, but also to cargo liners, fruit vessels, and special ships. One company, for instance, specialized in heavy lift-ships carrying locomotives in the hold, and railway passenger-carriages, light-ships, and barges on deck. Also, a hand-in-glove co-operation with Sweden had begun. Soon, 60% of the output of the Swedish shipyards was for Norwegians. Norway built in Denmark, too, and everywhere else, with the exception of Norway itself. By the turn of the century, her own ship-building had dwindled from a substantial figure to almost nothing.

'Shipowning is better than shipbuilding' says the Norwegian, as if this were undisputed. Shipyards and factories are rooted, while ships can move. A yard needed thousands of men, a ship only a handful. In a sense, this was paradoxical thinking, for it had always been stressed that Norwegian agriculture was of far greater importance than its earnings reflected, because it employed such a vast number of men, women, and children—the direct opposite of automation. From this point of view, one might have supposed that shipbuilding, not shipowning, would have been under-employed Norway's dream at the time.

The Norwegians sometimes overlooked the fact that profitable building was better than unprofitable owning. However, the truth remains that a shipyard is rather unwieldy and very much a limited liability company. An owner can venture out on his own as a 'Peer Gynt of the Waves'; he can be on his toes for lightning decisions if only he knows his business well enough to forecast with dead certainty. Tradition is not born in a day, and there are many fields where teamwork is imperative. The budding Norwegian shipowner could engage a complete chain of specialists—officers, men, superintendents, brokers—they were all there. Thus, owning is often better also for the country, although other countries may reap higher profits from building—for Norwegian owners.

Barren years followed 1929, and the world's harbours and estuaries were packed with rusting 'laid-ups'. And while other nations' ships were few *per capita,* and often a subventioned national insurance, Norway's ships were a heavily-taxed and good-sized portion of the national product and revenue. Exports cover only some two-thirds of the imports. The whole national standard would have had to be lowered if shipping-earnings had not filled the gap. The Norwegians advocated free international shipping. Cheaper freight rates spread the cheapest commodities over the globe. Flag discrimination and protected deficit fleets would have frustrated this and, incidentally, Norway, too.

During the slump, a world-wide tanker pool was created. 'Laid-ups' received compensation from those that were working. And so grave was the situation that demolition of all ships older than 25 years was suggested. This would have left one country with four ships out of 1½ million tons. Maybe this stroke of genius was Norwegian, since Norway's fleet was the world's youngest and the country was not in such a bad way. As a result of the 'corrosion scare' she had obtained the tanker profits, mostly long-term chartered. In the long run, genuine shipping benefits from economic slumps. Anyone can edge into a boom, and so-called 'bricklayers' shipping' ensues; yet slumps pare off outsiders. Many nations' fleets were operated by a handful of giant concerns, while Norway had hundreds of scattered companies, mostly with only one or two ships each. This was, in fact, a democratic approach on the cabin-boy-to-captain lines, an open school for shipping recruits, and a sound foundation for widespread specialization.

A shipyard contract should aim at the best combination of credit, quality, price, and building-time. Many nations may contend that they are the best shipbuilders, yet one owner may get a better ship than his competitor, who has out-of-date specifications. The Norwegians always paid very great attention to specifications, details of design and construction, so they could make their demands correspond to the requisite tonnage, whereas owners with inadequate specifications or old-standard 'handy vessels' failed. The Norwegians did not order, for instance, new coal-tramps; they knew that the coal-traffic was declining. Typical of the whole situation was the Norwegian near-monopoly in the St. Lawrence-Great Lakes trade with small boats with shallow draught, strengthened for ice and equipped for rounding tricky corners—in contrast to the rusty standard tramps lying idle elsewhere, whose owners had omitted to study the market and build better vessels to fit the trade. This was the era and vogue of the highly specialized cargo liners. Rudolf Diesel was not a Dane, but the first ocean-going diesel ship, *Selandia,* was built in Copenhagen in 1912. All innovations have their teething-troubles, but a diesel's higher initial cost was compensated by the lower fuel expenses. Also, the fewer liquid fuel tons could be stowed where no dry cargo could be stored, allowing the ship to take more freight, and also to avoid a number of bunkering calls. It was obvious for traditional coal countries to keep to steam-engines, even after the advent of liquid steam-engine fuel, although their vastly higher daily consumption of (cheaper) steam-engine fuel-oil—compared to diesel engine-oil—also stole tonnage and space. Less bound by tradition and with no coal mines, Scandinavia immediately embraced the competitive diesel; Norway rapidly acquired the world's highest diesel percentage and the largest fleet of independent tankers. The motor-tanker proved to be a happy combination of Norway's tanker and Denmark's motor-vessel.

Around the turn of the century, the sailing-ship builders and owners on the Norwegian south coast had gradually gone over to small steamers, but they hesitated to follow this up later with the larger ship-tanker trend. After a while Norway stagnated, and her sale of small shipping units decreased. The principal blame was put on her strict rules regarding overtime, minimum size of crew, and accommodation. Already in 1916 Norway had introduced a regulation providing for a maximum of two men per cabin. Another good reason was the fact that the Continent's extensive system of canal shipping had been motorized, with families living aboard the motor-barges. These barges had grown in size and seaworthiness and were beginning to travel much further down the Rhine than formerly into sectors of what was by tradition the North Sea trade of many nations. The Norwegians, with their social laws and higher running-expenses, were hardest hit. Norwegian North Sea sailors complained that this was not genuine competition on equal terms, but sweated foreign labour, and protested that the Dutch and German sailors ought to demand more men and higher pay. In the days when Norway prospered through hard work, good seamanship, and pluck, poems had been written about 'Glorious Norway', the survival of the fittest, free enterprise, and competition. However, when these same qualities and processes were turned against her, she called it despicable.

Hydro-electric industrialization, above all, had provided the Norwegians ashore with more posts and improved wages. Shipboard pay followed suit, and larger ships ran more cheaply with fewer men per ton. Conversely, small units needed higher freight-rates, and more men per ton. Germany and Holland were crowded countries suffering from unemployment. When Norway was invaded by Germany in 1940, she ranked—with nearly 5 million tons—fourth after Japan. In vain, Quisling ordered all ships to proceed to the nearest German or neutral port. Until the United States joined in, Norwegian tankers carried 40% of the petrol for the Battle of Britain. Churchill declared this fleet equal to an army of two million men.

The exiled Norwegian Government in London formed *Nortraship* for the management of all free vessels. The accruing freights gave them an income, in contrast to those of many other countries. This enabled Norway to pay her way independently, to man and run her own naval units, and to train an army in Scotland and airmen in Canada. During the war, the country lost many seamen. Half of the merchant fleet disappeared, and what remained was old and battered. At the end of the war everything was lacking in Norway, and rationing and severe currency restrictions were introduced. Reconstructing the merchant fleet seemed problematical.

Though the Norwegians had, in many ways, been better treated than other occupied nations, it was Norway's people who had to bear the brunt of the economic burdens. So, visualizing wholesale unemployment, the Norwegian Exile Government in London had, metaphorically speaking, prepared to send the whole nation into the forests with an axe each. They were back at the old-time agricultural approach of employing the highest possible number of persons. The influential generation of the day had suffered badly after 1929, and this still rankled. There was an urge for full employment as an aim in itself, to allay the horror of unemployment they dreaded. Even in maritime Norway, the shipping and sea-faring community formed only a very small minority of a nation of 'landlubbers', whose hearts never went out greatly in sympathy to the 'men of the brine'. A shipowner was a Ltd. employee, but the 'one-man show' was such that people were aware of the man himself, not of his company, in contrast to the factory-manager of any well-known firm. People said textile *industry,* but ship*owner*— a symbol of personal success and a public life—uplifted, glorified, and doubtlessly envied.

Moreover, most people in Norway saw high-geared shipping finance as a dangerous source of debt. They thought all the nation's resources at sea and ashore should be pooled and the number of highly speculative ships, which also employed comparatively few people, should be reduced. Why did not the shipowners invest in shore industries instead? The opposite stand was to make one pool of all shore activities, and the shipping business into another pool, distinct from the shore economy. Shipping could not invest ashore because the whole idea of high-geared finance lay in the charterer's procuring or gilt-edging practically all the investments. The oil companies would not invest in Norwegian firms ashore, and no financial institutions would lend at such high percentages to shore enterprises. High-geared shipping loans could be obtained, irrespective of what the country could produce. The whole political economic debate in Norway since the war has shuttled between these two extremes.

Considerable capital was invested in shipyards, for currency restrictions barred investment of Norwegian money in foreign ships, even though a Norwegian-built 18,000-ton ship cost as much as a foreign 24,000-ton vessel, with additional building-time and interest. Disgruntled shipping men argued that they could earn capital faster than any other enterprise if they were left to their own devices, and could thus be of service to industry and consumption at home. The Government (Labour from 1936), they added, saw the national earnings as one lump, irrespective of its origin, to be equitably redistributed to consumers and industries of all kinds. Shipping alleged that it was detrimental to the whole national economy if foreign exchange from shipping, instead of being ploughed back into shipping again to bring in further capital, was used to support activities unconnected with shipping. On the other hand, shore industrialists complained that shipping was privileged enough already. Irritation was further roused by the very visible cars and nylons of the shipping people, for strict rationing was still in force: textiles till 1951, cars till 1959.

In contrast to the Norwegian seamen, many foreign crews accepted payment in domestic currency, with the exception of a small sum for shore-leave abroad. The Norwegians could choose any currency, even dollars, at a special rate. 'We create hard exchange and are entitled to it', was their attitude. This was erroneous, since shore labour, which produced exports or import-saving articles, received no compensation.

The case was not comparable with that of Dutch or British sailors, for example, who served mostly in shipping between the motherland and overseas, with their own language, beer, and compatriots at either end. The Norwegians were plying between foreign ports for 80% of the time, with perhaps a five-year period in Asia. Obviously such sailors should have the right to claim international pay. 'Why should we have to pay taxes for pavements we never see?' they argued. The greyness of Norway in the 'hydro-electric age' had made the young Norwegians used to the thought of expatriation as a natural thing. For more than a century, Norwegians had settled in Wisconsin, Minnesota, and the Dakotas, and had manned Norwegian and other ships. American ships paid better, too, and in dollars.

This international wage was granted, not so much perhaps in fairness, as because the seamen were in a position to demand it. Traditionally, barren granite shores had compelled the Norwegian sailor to accept a humble hire, since it was a case of 'Hobson's choice'. Now, for the first time he could make demands. This was due partly to the new industries, which drew labour away from agriculture and forestry. While agriculture used to employ the highest number of hands, the figure is now down to 14% of the national labour-force, and industry has increased by more than double this figure. Many young people from the coast took employment in factories just for the novelty of having freedom of choice. On the other hand, the mountain lad bent on going to sea had found no berth in the old days, when innate boatmanship was imperative, but with the new labour shortage and shipboard tasks becoming more and more similar to shore work, such positions are now open to him. Ships are being increasingly manned from the farming counties and northern fishing communities.

After the war, Norway's imports had grossly exceeded her exports, and the gap had to be bridged. There was a widespread opinion that the post-war shipping boom would soon be over, and that the national resources would have to be harnessed for full employment and compensatory activities. In 1948, the Government laid an embargo on the import of ships. Shipping circles still thought that their experts knew best, however, and held to their own opinion. 'You politicians', they said in effect, 'see only a national deficit and staggering ship import figures; and you are trying to save the country by killing the goose that lays the golden eggs.'

Then the foreign oil-industry asked long-established Norwegian shipping partners to supply more tankers, and the shipowners had regretfully to decline. They could not do it in consequence of the embargo, they apologized. As the oil-industry needed tonnage to satisfy its growing requirements, it was compelled to contact owners who had never done any tankering before and who knew nothing of high-geared finance shipping. British passenger lines assumed some of the oil, but the bulk of this huge and lucrative business was taken by Americans and Greeks living in exile in America. They registered under the flags of Panama, Liberia, and Honduras—'Panhonlib'. The 'Stars and Stripes' was out of the question owing to prohibitive wages. Once these newcomers were established, no one could oust them again. Norwegian shipping circles soon complained that this state of affairs had cost Norway a thousand million Kroner. And even two years after the embargo was lifted, each owner had to borrow

100% of the cost of the foreign ship in his own good name in order to get a ship import permit.

In the late 'twenties the Norwegian formula had been 'knowledge, oil, shipyard', which worked satisfactorily. This pooling of interests had demonstrated that impecunious experts could be trusted with ships, but it had resulted mainly in creating 'small new colleagues' for the existing great shipowners in Norway. On the other hand, old and reliable companies in Norway and in other countries clung doggedly to economy shipping—even to the extent of paying for the ship in full on signature of the shipyard contract. They obtained the ships cheap, because they themselves financed the yard. Disregarding finance and contracting shipping, they shouldered all the risks, in accordance with the old truth that what a free-lance gains during a boom would balance his losses during a slump, and express itself in higher percentage dividends on a relatively small, unencumbered fleet.

But if it was a fact that a clerk could be metamorphosed into the owner of a single vessel with a 90% debt based on a long-term pre-construction oil-company charter, it was also conceivable that he could grow and one day equal the fleet, salary, and percentages of the cash-down owner. Of course, the orthodox company owning ten debt-free ships could, using the same method, procure 100 ships on a 90% credit; but it was in the very nature of their mentality that they would not do so. In such a case, the established high-geared finance companies would overtake them in size, and new companies would be founded. Although this whole approach still remained an incomprehensible riddle to many, it became internationally known. There were scores who wanted to join in, and the general post-war development was such that it could take place on a much larger scale.

Panhonlib owners exploded into mammoth operators, and their meteoric rise has been argued in proof of the magnitude of Norway's losses. This magnitude, however, proves something else. From 1926 onwards, the Norwegians had built up a virtual monopoly of independent tankers, and they still held this unique trump card after 1945. The cry for tanker tonnage was so loud, however, that Norway could not possibly have raised means and men for it all. While the oil trade quintupled between 1939 and 1960, the world tanker fleet grew from 11 to 41 million tons. Newcomers would sooner or later have forced their way in. The Norwegian embargo had merely precipitated the inevitable. Although there was an unmistakable boom in shipping, it rode partly on the wave of the questionable Korean war. Norway also developed a more balanced economy by means of, for instance, the production of aluminium. The ship import restrictions helped the new or expanding shipyards overcome their initial difficulties. Today, like world shipping, they are somewhat over-developed, but the industry is sound and up-to-date, and supplies one-fourth of Norway's needs, that is, upward of 590,000 annual gross tons. Norway is now eighth in rank as a shipbuilding nation, and she even exports ships.

Soon after the war, despite all the restrictions, the Norwegian fleet had regained its 1939 size, and by 1955 it had grown to seven million tons. Non-shipping circles deemed this tonnage too high and considered it a danger. Shipping circles retorted that the pre-war tonnage had been 7% of the world total and that seven million tons fell far short of this figure.

There was still apparently sympathy for shipyards, a tendency to view the combination of owning and building as a two-hundred-per-cent business, if all Norwegian ships had to be 100% Norwegian built. Disregarding the fact that such a view had lost Great Britain and the United States a hegemony, it is a mistaken idea. Does a cabby necessarily have to build his own taxi? This contradicts the Norwegian approach to shipping. Ships should compete freely in distributing products from all parts of the world in the best and cheapest way. Shipping services are an exchangeable form of merchandise, and an efficient service demands the best and cheapest ships, whether they are Norwegian or not. The main objection, however, is to the fact that shipowning and shipbuilding is considered to be a two-hundred-per-cent business. It is, in fact, a one-hundred-per-cent business. The same coin cannot buy twice! Norway's problem has always been, still is, and will always remain a scarcity of capital. If local yards supply 10% of the tonnage needs, and politicians desire to step this up to 20%, this may actually reduce the merchant fleet. Without enough capital to go round, it would be necessary to rob Peter to pay Paul.

Modern wealth does not result simply from increased production, but rather from having relatively fewer people to share it, by reason of more and better equipment, automation, and family-planning. In Norway, shipowning was always better as a profit-earner than merely as an employer of the unemployed. In the over-employed or under-populated Norway of today, capital in a ship with 60 men is better than in a shipyard with 1000, if only for the reason that the other 940 can be employed wherever their labour is needed. This does not mean that shipbuilding should be restricted when it is able to compete; capital would be found for both the present fleet and for the shipyards. Nevertheless, Norway specializes in owning, Sweden in building. On the whole, Sweden's yards are probably the most efficient in the world today, and in spite of paying the highest wages in Europe, they remain powerful competitors. Only Japan is building more cheaply, though admittedly with lower wages. Japan has also adopted highly rationalized shipbuilding methods, and, as a result of her sensational upsurge, she is now far ahead of all other shipbuilding countries.

Still today, the yacht that wins the America Cup is more than just the combined effect of science, crew, and money. Not many decades ago, the same applied to commercial vessels. Today, commercial shipbuilding is international knowledge. Competition criteria are quality, credit, price, building-time, and, to some extent, the owners' specifications. For the most part, the type designs and the details of construction of the individual yards are accepted. In general, Norwegian owners managed to finance further expansion of their fleets, but some of them 'missed the boat'—on account of their conservatism and the restrictions. Also the growing size of ships meant colossal expenditure. The highly-specialized cargo liners, lucrative between the wars, were becoming too expensive, yet they continued to carry cargo. Some owners, for example, had an 18,000-ton tanker, a good income, a ship entirely written off, but a new ship of the same type might cost about three times as much, and they would need a much larger ship in order to compete at all. Tankers had grown to over 20,000 tons, and people spoke of 33,000-ton supertankers! An international enterprise, in co-operation with an Arab oil sheik, ordered 50,000-ton ships. Many Norwegian owners were not in a position to finance a ship of the size they knew they must have. Until quite recently, the Norwegian fleet included many new units which were already technically obsolete. The Norwegians simply could not compete with supertankers.

If reasonable-sized ships had formerly given the shipping-clerk a chance to become an owner, it was now a question of no longer being able to do so, or of investing in ships costing millions of pounds sterling. This favoured the existing big firms, choked the recruiting of new owners, and 'mammothed' Panhonlibs—until Liberia for a short while overtook Norway as number 3.

And Norway could no longer find enough Norwegian crews, so that the old prejudice against women had to be dropped and they were allowed to work on the ships, changing the tone altogether—saloon girls, female galley crews, and wireless operators—sometimes nicknamed 'La Sparks'. Married couples sought ship jobs, and members of the crew got married. Today there are about 4,000 women working aboard Norwegian ships. Foreign nationals were also hired. Liners took on Goans for galley and passenger service. Scores of ships out East, also tankers in international trade, had Norwegian officers, the rest of the crew being Chinese. Norwegian ships were filled with Displaced Persons, Spaniards, Belgians, Britons, and Swiss. Norway's 1½ million tons in the 'eighties had employed as many Norwegians as her present 18 million tons from an almost doubled population—43,000 Norwegians, 14,000 of other nationalities. Sea-faring Norway is going ashore, while Norway's shipping is growing as never before.

The orthodox approach to owning had been to work for a net surplus after the deduction of income-tax, and for the highest interest possible in ready cash. With better telecommunications, however, the super-sensitive shipping needle trembled second by second to fluctuations in world trade caused by inflation, drought, rain, cold, heat, wars, changing populations and politics. To plan and build a ship takes time. Playing the international market means constantly keeping a finger on the pulse of world markets—no guesswork, no gambling. With the enormous capital required for the steadily increasing size of the ships, an owner, however outstanding in day-to-day operations he may be, would lose to the one who, possibly with less resources at his command, is better informed and has a good critical judgement, so that he will order the right kind of ship with the right specifications at the right time and at an advantageous price.

A cheaper ship means better running economy. More important, however, is the tax-free direct step-up in capital, in many cases far above what could be otherwise earned in many years of plodding. The art of ship-contracting has brought the financial aspect to the fore. Many such owners felt that they must make the most of global conjunctures, leaving everything else to a shipping agency.

The Norwegian tonnage grew rapidly and the south coast became dynamic again. In the late 'fifties, the Norwegian fleet approached 10% of the world fleet. Ships of

33,000 tons were no longer considered 'super'—ships of 100,000 tons were being designed. Today, units of 130,000 tons or more are trading or being built, and Japan is going to build seven shipyards, five of which will be capable of producing ships of 150,000 tons or more. The designs of ships for the transport of dry cargo has been revised. The bridge-structure has been combined with the engine casing and moved aft, together with the engine, as in a tanker, shortening the long propeller-shaft and hold-tunnel. Decks are now clear of superstructure: rail-cranes can perambulate the ship's length and replace the traditional derricks. The United States, whose labour is expensive, has abolished shore cranes. It is more practical to drive fork-lifters through side gates and stack whole loads in the hold. There have been combined ships—oil one way, ore return. Special tankers have been designed for liquefied petroleum gases, or for molten sulphur at 250° C. Tankers have been adapted for bulk grain. Wholesale ship automation is now setting in, with a drastic reduction of crew.

Tankers, the carriers of liquid bulk, had set an example in pre-construction charter, multi-interest combined-ships, and increased size. In spite of having the same parts, the 'tanker idea' was not transferred to ships for dry bulks, which were still handled by traditional half-size tramps, or even vacant liners. While the oil concerns are few but large, and oil-ports at both ends are few, any amount of dry cargo is carried both to and from a great number of shallow harbours.

It was the gigantic rise in the shipping of minerals and raw materials of all kinds which pushed modern ship designs in the direction of the tanker model. Up to a point, a big ship was a small one enlarged. Few additional men were called for, and the engine did not have to be powered up in proportion to the increased load. Modern technics had deepened harbours, and they could be dredged even deeper. Larger ships could make both ends meet despite lower rates, but could not easily be chartered through the brokers for single trips. The tanker-combine had to be copied. For example, a Brazilian mine can contact its Japanese customers, whose Government wants the ships built and owned in Japan, who cannot finance both. It is proposed to finance internationally a 60,000-ton ship, to be built in Japan, possibly with some Brazilian and some Japanese stock, to be operated by Japan on a long-term charter at a lower rate of freight. This is mutual assistance. Everybody benefits, including the consumer, who gets the metal cheaper.

So now giant bulk-carriers are ploughing the seas, looking like tankers, unless you know the difference. In this field the Norwegians have done a great deal. Today, they own some four million tons dead weight, and are second after Liberia, but by only a narrow margin.

Norwegian shipping began with home ships, crews, owners, brokers, and flag, for local trade, and developed into a service that spans the world. Ships were imported and foreign crews engaged, but flag, broker, and owner remained Norwegian. This development has made the sailor independent of the owner, and *vice versa*. Shipwork can now be done by people from the interior of the country, with no knowledge of the sea, and therefore by international crews. Crews depend upon the ship. The owner is responsible for both their jobs and his own, wherever his office-buildings may be, which is not necessarily in Norway itself. Most Norwegian capital has been raised on world finance's belief in a certain person; a number of shipping experts could, just for the sake of argument, have emigrated from Norway in 1945 to a country without currency and other restrictions, could have settled elsewhere, and procured the same financial resources there—and another flag could have fluttered over the present Norwegian fleet. Many could have quintupled their present companies. They stayed in Norway, however, because, after the German occupation, their country developed into a peaceful democracy, where shipping could be carried on. There were other countries where this was not the case.

Part of the colossal war-built United States merchant marine has been mothballed as a defense reserve. In addition to the Army, Navy, and Air Force—and because the American wages have made competitive shipping impossible—substantial merchant shipping has been subsidized to the ceiling which United States tax-payers could be expected to bear, as an ever-ready national safety stand-by. To procure the rest of the merchant fleet which the United States authorities deemed a safety minimum, they have more or less officially encouraged American owners to register Panhonlib. In this way, the ships would be as easily available as the American ships, but paying their unsubsidized way in consequence of much lower running-expenses. This idea of a 'fifth arm' excludes Panhonlib ships not owned by United States citizens, as well as those sailing under flags other than that of Panhonlib.

The Greek case was parallel, but not identical. Eminent Greek shipping men in Great Britain and Greece had made money before Greece became entangled in the war, but the post-war upheavals made shipping under the Greek flag more than problematical. International finance even declined loans to shipping sailing under the Greek flag. Already in 1946, Greek shipping men had bought over 600,000 tons of United States surplus tonnage; and since their own flag acted as a deterrent, they registered under Panhonlib. They went over to tankers, and more Greeks joined them, particularly after the Norwegian ship import embargo in 1948.

'Normal' flag companies are taxed, whether they intend to pay dividends or not. If they pay dividends, at least one United States Panhonlib owner must pay regular United States taxes, but if the dividends are withheld, the whole surplus can be switched to expansion without taxation. Owing to these company tax freedom advantages, these flags are called 'flags of convenience' or 'flags of necessity', the latter frequently being just another way of saying 'flag of convenience'—an attempt to white-wash what is obnoxious. However, convenience means seeking an attractive flag, necessity means avoiding an unpopular one. From the outset, the 40% American and 45% Greek Panhonlib participation, equalling 85%, sailed under flags that were not their own national ones for either economic or political reasons, or both, in order to avoid insurmountable handicaps, and not in order to derive advantages, either fair or unfair. The tax-free Panhonlib operation was, of course, a stroke of luck for them; and even if the terms 'flag of necessity' and 'flag of convenience' are confusing, it does not prevent shipowners from enjoying both. Registration with Panhonlib was primarily a necessity; convenience was secondary and, as it were, coincidental. If Panhonlib had not existed, both groups would have sought other 'normal' flags and registered, for example, in those traditional shipping countries which had overlooked the chance offered them by the Norwegian embargo, and which had failed to take advantage of the world's need for tonnage.

There was a tonnage gap, and the owners who might have been expected to fill it were either not allowed to do so, or else they would not or could not. These New York Greeks and Americans (one was of Norwegian origin) were subject to none of those exchange restrictions, and various others which hampered other nations. Living on the spot in the city of skyscrapers, where everything is within reach, they could catch the faintest rumour and seize a good business opportunity without having to fill in forms or await the decision of the authorities.

From 1926 onwards, the independent tanker market was in the hands of London and Norway, Norway being the centre because the oil companies sought Norwegian owners in an otherwise reluctant market. Since 1945, both the surplus ship market and the finance market have been concentrated largely in New York, even if the tanker centre lingered on in Norway, since oil still sought its traditional shipping partners—until the Norwegian Government embargoed ship imports in 1948, and Norway was forced back on to the periphery.

Gradually, other flags adopted various equalizing measures, such as a 40% investment allowance, a high depreciation allowance if dividends were renounced, a tax-free Bermuda Company sailing under the British flag with lower wages than would have been paid under the Bermuda or Panhonlib flags, and so on. And to attract crews, ships under the Panhonlib or the Bermuda flag had to raise their wages. The Panhonlib social and other laws were weak, but world finance protected itself by seeing to it that its collateral factors were in order and unobjectionable. Greece also made her flag attractive, whereupon huge transfers of Panhonlib tonnage nearly raised her into the front rank, while Liberia lost by it. It is something of a paradox that it was just Greece that obtained this impressive fleet, which could never have been created in Greece itself.

Panhonlib owners have also registered under many other flags, the Norwegian among them. Norwegian owners have recently placed about one-third of the world orders for ships—a fact which is jocularly argued to prove that Norway is today a 'convenience country'. Panhonlib owners, they say, have no advantages. But all the negative factors take effect only after they have actually enjoyed great advantages, and have acquired their mammoth fleets. Modern construction favours the great, and they had certainly grown rapidly great from 1946 onwards.

This intricate complication involved world shipping in a debate in which it is hard to distinguish the emotional from the factual. The true picture will probably emerge only when all this has become past history—and what has been said above can do no more than hint at what is going on. There is more to the story than the simplified version that, with grossly unfair advantages, a mere name-plate, and no genuine link with the flag under which they sail, bogus fleets are pirating genuine maritime concerns, and so are responsible for the over-tonnage in the world today and, as a result, for a long shipping slump.

What would Norwegian shipping have done if the currency restrictions which began in 1945, and the 1948 embargo, had never been? Would it have made a difference if Norwegian owners had moved to New York after 1945, leaving their companies in Norway? Norwegians have recently stated that it is increasingly necessary to be where the markets are. Jet aviation may be helping them to feel the pulse on the spot. At least they have made a fantastic come-back, both in tankers and bulk carriers. Though a slump existed for years, their fleet expanded, and, a large part of the tonnage being long-term chartered, the national loss on the rest of the fleet was made good by additional ships, and the total income again increased.

Exactly the same thing is happening today, and warning fingers are again being held up. Maybe they are right this time, but it still remains to be seen. A large proportion of the world's shipbuilding contracts are for Norwegian owners—whatever this may mean to the age, type, size, quality of the ships, their profitability, and the change in percentage rates. In 1963, Norway acquired 1 3/4 million gross tons of new ships, a net increase of about a million tons. The difference includes a corrective of that period some time ago, when 'progressive memory' was to some extent lacking. This fascinating game is only possible for those who feel: 'The world is my village'—not 'My village is the world'.

What will be the future of Norway's shipping business? A forecast is possible only on the basis of past experience. The Norwegian will order the most suitable type of ships at the most advantageous prices, built to the best specifications for his shipping trade, and he will order at the right moment. He will carry all kinds of merchandise and will cross-trade in an International Common Market, to everybody's benefit—including his own.

Hans Geelmuyden

80 Fishing-cutter off the North Cape massif, on Mageröy

81 Beacon near Helnes, on the outer Porsanger Fjord

82 The North Cape
83, 84, 85 With the Lapps at Karasjok, not far from Porsanger Fjord

84

86 Lapp tent with watch-dog
87 Midnight sun ▷

The Lapps

The Lapps of Norway are a particular group of people within the native population. Numerically, they are a minority of some 20,000 persons living in scattered groups from Lake Femunden in southern Norway up to the Arctic Ocean in the north. A further 13,000 Lapps live outside the Norwegian borders, namely, in Sweden, Finland, and the Soviet Union.

Although the great majority of the Lapps live in such a modern state as Norway, they have only been partially assimilated by the population of that country. An encounter with these singular inhabitants is, at all events, an interesting experience. We are thinking especially of the nomadic Lapps, but even in the case of many sedentary Lapps we find a way of life entirely different from that of the Scandinavian peoples.

The Mountain Lapps

The Norwegian Lapps may be called a people of mountain and fjord. Those most closely connected with the mountains are known as the reindeer or mountain Lapps. Although they constitute a mere 10% of the Lapp population of Norway, they are nevertheless found all over Lapp-inhabited Norwegian territory. We also differentiate between river Lapps, who live on the shores of the lakes and rivers in the heart of Finnmark, and sea Lapps, who have settled round the fjords of Finnmark and in other areas of the extreme north. A fourth group, the forest Lapps, are resident mainly in Sweden; they also have herds of reindeer, which, however, are mostly smaller and tamer than those of the nomadic Lapps.

The mountain or nomadic Lapps have the most typical characteristics of the various groups of Norwegian Lapps; it is they who have best preserved the ancient cultural heritage of Lapland. They are the closest to Nature, and the old Lapp occupation of reindeer breeding has contributed towards preserving their language and costume.

The Lapps have hundreds of names for the reindeer, according to the sex, age, colour, form, shape of the antlers, tameness, and characteristics as a worker. The highly-specialized Lapp vocabulary also extends, for example, to the various aspects of tending the reindeer herds, to migration and migration routes, to pastures, the equipment of the herdsmen, their tents and turf huts. The language illustrates the ancient community of Lapp and reindeer, giving a picture of the high standard which his breeding methods have attained today.

The relatively long migration distances are typical of the reindeer herding activities of the mountain Lapps. The transfer of their reindeer herds from one pasture to another takes place according to a given cycle, which allows for the fodder requirements of the animals during the various seasons of the year. In summer they sojourn in areas with a rich variety of grasses and herbs, and in winter at places where the animals can dig through the snow to the lichen.

In Finnmark, the nomadic Lapps and their reindeer herds spend the summer on the coast or in the high mountains of the interior and, during the winter, in forests or their immediate vicinity. In southern regions, however, the best winter pastures are to be found not far from the coast, and the best summer ones near the Swedish border. Maximum migration-distances of 400 kilometres (c. 150 miles) occur in Finnmark. In the following pages we shall try to depict a nomadic Lapp family in this region, whose way of life is deeply rooted in tradition.

Today, in spite of the fact that the Lapps' reindeer breeding is subject to the laws of development, one still finds families who have retained the intrinsic features of an older way of life. The three essential requisites of this trade are the herdsman's dog, the lasso, and skis. A number of castrated male reindeer are used for drawing sleds and carrying loads. For winter transport in trackless regions, the Lapp has employed, from time immemorial, a most suitable sled. It has one runner and looks like a rowing-boat cut in half; it is called a *geris* and was presumably adopted from the ancestors of the Finns. The type varies according to whether it is employed as a passenger or a transport vehicle. Its pointed shape facilitates progress in forest and thicket. In sparsely-wooded areas, the Finnish sled with two runners has been introduced in more recent times.

On migration, the tent was indispensable for the Lapp. It has a framework of light construction which can be easily transported on an open sled. Apart from straight upright poles, this framework consists of two pairs of curved or forked poles which are joined to horizontal tent-poles, thus affording greater space inside the tent. This version of the Lapp tent is the family's winter abode. The reindeer herdsmen generally use the simpler tent, which has only straight poles. In summer, it serves at the same time as the family home and has the advantage that the heavy curved poles need not be transported to the summer pastures. The tent-cloth, which is in two parts, is fastened at the back and at the front. On entering the Lapp's tent for the first time, one may receive the impression of a certain disorder. This disorder is, however, only apparent. In actual fact, strict order reigns. The floor is divided into five sections and covered with twigs. Beyond the tent door, the visitor steps across the wood-pile; then comes the fireplace, or hearth, surrounded by stones, and, in the innermost part, we find the kitchen section with cooking utensils and other requisites. In earlier times, this part and the place behind the Lapp tent were regarded as holy, and taboos were laid upon them. A captured bear, for instance, was always brought in by the secret 'back door'. According to traditional belief, it would then be unable to find its way on returning to avenge itself. Reindeer are slaughtered behind the tent. On either side of the fireplace is the tent-dwellers' sitting and sleeping accommodation; this is often marked out with wooden logs. Reindeer skins serve as mattresses. There is no furniture in the Lapp tent, the space being insufficient. Apart from the cooking utensils, we may find a couple of wooden boxes and a chest. During the day, the bed-covers and articles of clothing are rolled up and stowed near the wall of the tent, where they also serve as a protection against draughts, and on the tent-poles there are wooden and horn hooks. The smoke-hole is directly over the hearth.

In winter, the fire in the Lapp tent burns the whole day and, if possible, during the night as well. If it goes out, the temperature inside the tent sometimes falls to 30° to 40° C. below zero. In the case of low temperatures such as these, sleep becomes difficult even for the Lapp, although he can bear extreme cold and fluctuations of temperature better than most. When the wind blows through the smoke-hole, the smoke from the open fire becomes a nuisance, and the older Lapps frequently have red-rimmed, watery eyes.

A Lapp camp generally comprises several family-tents. Various Lapp families unite according to old custom and work together. A reindeer camp of this type is called a *siida*. The members of this *siida* choose a leader, the *siida-isid* or 'reindeer camp chief'. The *siida,* as a community, is completely democratic, and each member is free to join another *siida* if he choses to do so.

The main occupation of the reindeer herder is tending the animals. Both men and women have taken part in this task for generations. The work of a herdsman is arduous, and involves great responsibility, especially in winter; for at that time of year, the wolf and the glutton, or wolverine, are a constant danger to the reindeer. Should the herd be attacked by beasts of prey and scatter, it is often extremely difficult to retrieve the terrified animals.

A further danger for the reindeer in winter is the ice-crust which forms on the pastures after a thaw and prevents the animals from reaching the lichen. It is then often impossible to keep the reindeer under control in their search for food. The members of the various reindeer camps share the duties of tending the herds, the times being exactly prescribed. The herdsmen use skis in winter, skirting the pasture area at daybreak, in search of tracks of runaway reindeer. The missing animals must at all costs be re-captured.

When pasture conditions are favourable and the region is not rendered unsafe by beasts of prey, winter is a comparatively peaceful time for the nomadic Lapps. With the advent of spring, in April, a new life begins for them, and with the spring migration in the second half of the month, the most arduous phase of the working year sets in. The main thing is to get the female reindeer which are in calf to the calving-locality as fast as possible. At this time, the female reindeer hurry instinctively, while the male animals and the young ones take their time; they are often herded along with the others. During the prevailing mild weather, the snow is mostly wet and heavy in the daytime, freezing at night. For this reason, the families rest during the day and move on during the night, thus saving time and effort. The stages of the journey are long, so that both man and beast are almost exhausted on arrival at their destination places.

The reindeer calving-place is selected with care and usually retained for years. It must be as sheltered as possible from wind and weather, and there must be no danger to the young animals, such as steep precipices, in the vicinity. At the same time, the location must assure adequate fodder for the very difficult transition period between winter and summer.

As a rule, the reindeer start calving at the beginning of May. Immediately after the birth, the young animal is licked dry by its mother, which prevents it from freezing. The calf soon stands on its own legs and is already able to follow its mother when barely two hours old. A few days later, it can already run faster than a man. During the birth, the reindeer must be left to herself as much as possible and must not be frightened. The duty of the herdsman during this phase consists in observing the animals from a distance and protecting them from all danger.

When migrating to the calving-locations, the Lapps use sleds loaded with all the requisite luggage. The sleds, harnessed to reindeer, are drawn up into a long line, called a *raido* in the Lapp language. In this *raido,* in which every type of sled has its specified place, each reindeer is attached to the sled in front of it. A few Lapp families choose the summer pasture-land as the calving-location, and so can drive their sleds straight through to their new destination. For others, these places are situated at varying distances from the summer pastures, and the last stage of the spring migration, after the reindeer have calved, leads for the most part through regions more or less free from snow. In this case, the sled is replaced by pack-saddles and the reindeer carry the baggage on their backs, the pack-loads, which must not weigh more than 30–40 kilogrammes (about 15–20 pounds) in all!, being evenly distributed on either side. On its arrival at the summer pasture, the reindeer has usually become very thin; but the wholesome and nourishing plants of the summer pasture-land strengthen the animals in a short time, permitting them to store the necessary calory-reserves for the privations of a hard winter, with its one-sided diet of reindeer-moss.

The amount of work which the reindeer entails for the Lapp differs according to whether he is in the high mountains of the interior or on the sea-shore. In the interior, there are fewer natural obstacles to keep the herds together. Thus the animals are under the herdsman's supervision day and night. On islands and peninsulas, this duty is obviated on account of the natural bounds set by the sea. Today, in many peninsular locations, fenced enclosures are erected to prevent the reindeer from breaking away to other pastures. As a sign of ownership, the Lapp marks his animals' ears. Each reindeer owner has an officially registered personal mark. The marking consists of incisions of varying shapes, each shape having its own designation. These incisions are combined in a special way by the individual Lapp. As the animal is marked on both ears, the marking variants are extremely numerous. By being able to recognize certain distinctive features, such as the colour of the coat and the shape of the antlers, the nomadic Lapp has exceptional skill at quickly picking out his own animals from a herd of several hundred reindeer. The reindeer is marked while still a calf. As the cutting of the ears during the winter can lead to frost-bite, the Lapp does the marking in summer. In earlier times, the female reindeer was also milked during the summer. However, the development of reindeer breeding, which has resulted in ever larger herds, has compelled the Lapp to limit his milking activities, which have, today, been given up completely by most breeders. For this reason, the reindeer are no longer so tame as they used to be. The milk-yield of the reindeer is small, but the milk has a high fat content and consequently a high nutritive value. It used to be made into cheese in little bowls of plaited roots and ornamented wooden moulds. This reindeer cheese was either used by the Lapps in their own households or employed as a medium of barter for the acquisition of commodities outside the *siida*.

The duties incumbent upon the Lapps during the summer half-year include the castration of the male reindeer. This operation is performed for several reasons. Firstly, the Lapp is then sure of having fattened beasts available, for the uncastrated reindeer lose a great deal of weight during the autumn rutting-season. Castration also involves a pre-selection for breeding purposes, the sturdiest males being exempted. Finally, the Lapps tame a number of castrated male reindeer as working animals. In earlier times, castration was performed by chewing the testicles, which virtually excluded the danger of infection. This method, which is apparently very old, since it was practised by other reindeer-breeding peoples, has recently been forbidden. Today, castration is performed with specially-constructed forceps.

In late summer, the Lapps start assembling their animals for the autumn migration. It often happens that the animals mix with those of other communities during the course of the summer, and they must therefore be sorted. The Lapps drive their animals to a certain spot of ground, where the 'foreign' reindeer are lassoed and then returned to their own herds. The reindeer used formerly to be much tamer than they are today, and the lasso sufficed to recapture them, but now circular corrals connected with small enclosures are constructed. The reindeer are herded into the larger corral, where the various owners recapture their truant animals with the lasso and haul them into the smaller enclosures. Reindeer that belong to the same herd are thus assembled in one place. This sorting must be repeated at certain intervals. Towards the end of summer, the reindeer begin to put on weight, and the slaughtering-season begins. Slaughtering takes place at intervals during the autumn, and the number killed is determined by the requirements of the breeder. During the course of the autumn slaughtering-season, stocks of meat are also laid in for late winter and spring, for the reindeer lose so much weight in the winter that further slaughtering in the spring would be unprofitable.

Migration begins in September. The reindeer camps withdraw by stages to the winter pasture-land. The rutting-season commences halfway through the month, and the Lapps interrupt migration for several weeks until the mating season is over. During this period, the reindeer, who have their particular rutting places, are also left to themselves, but they remain under the watchful eye of the herdsman. After the mating season is over, the reindeer communities set off again, reaching their winter quarters around Christmas.

In earlier times, the reindeer supplied the Lapp family with almost all the food it required. The entire animal was utilized: the meat, suet, blood, chitterlings, and marrow bones served as food, while the skin was made into clothes, sewing-thread being obtained by fraying out and retwining the sinews. Utensils such as lasso-rings, spoons, needle-cases, and awls were made of horn and bone. Fish, berries, and herbs supplemented this diet. The Lapps bartered reindeer meat, reindeer cheese, and reindeer skins with farmers and traders for flour, salt, sugar, tobacco, and textiles. More skins used to be exchanged for other commodities than is the case today.

In recent times, currency has replaced the system of barter in mountain Lapp trading, thus greatly changing their way of life. Roads have been built to the Lapp centres of Kautokeino, Karasjok, and Polmak. The state-built slaughter-houses and refrigeration-plants are also situated in these villages. The meat is transported in heavy trucks to the coast or by inland routes to the great market-centres of southern Norway. The Lapps have come to expect far more of life than they did a few years ago. Motorcycles and cars also find many buyers among their number and practically every Lapp family owns a radio. With regard to fashions, too, there are marked changes among them, and, above all in summer, the clothing of many of them differs in no way whatever from that of their Scandinavian neighbours.

As far as his home is concerned, the Lapp's demands have likewise increased. Many nomadic Lapps now build themselves houses in the vicinity of school and church; this serves as a place of permanent winter residence for their families, while the grown men or paid herdsmen rove about with the reindeer herds. When the children's school-holidays begin in the spring, the entire Lapp family often sets out for the summer pasture-land. Here they still live in tents or turf huts, although even in these summer pasture regions quite a number of houses are already to be seen.

The continued adaptation of the Lapps to modern conditions has been largely responsible for the change in the original character of reindeer-breeding in Finnmark. The traditions of payment in kind and the barter of goods have lost their place as the corner-stone of the Lapp economy. Hunting, fishing, and agriculture are also geared to finance, and a kind of semi-nomadism is replacing the traditional nomadism. This development is not confined to Finnmark alone, but can be observed in all Lapp regions.

Today, the Norwegian Lapp reindeer-breeders are united in a professional organization, forming a union like all the other trade-groups of the country. This organization has already rendered valuable service in the interests of its members. Reindeer-breeding in the Far North is largely dependent on the weather and therefore exposed to serious risks. The reindeer are sensitive to changes in the weather, prone to sickness, and constantly endangered by wild animals. An unfortunate concatenation of circumstances can ruin a wealthy Lapp in a short space of time, as he has no means of insuring his herd against loss or injury. One of the main objectives of the professional organization is to create a form of collective insurance in order to give relief in cases of severe hardship. The attainment of this aim would represent a great advantage for the Lapps, as well as for the country as a whole, for the utilization of the country's extensive untillable mountain region for reindeer-breeding lies very much in the interest of the Norwegian economy.

The River Lapps

This group of Lapps has settled principally in the vicinity of rivers and lakes in central Finnmark. Many river Lapps originally lived on the coast, but then wandered inland; some of them are descended from former nomads who gave up reindeer-herding. Agriculture and fishing are their main occupations; they also hunt, fell trees, and gather berries. In some cases, they engage in transport. Earlier, their main source of income was hunting and fishing, while cultivation of the soil was a side-line. Agriculture was carried on by primitive methods until the Second World War, and the river Lapps obtained fodder for their animals from bogs and meadows with the aid of home-made implements. After the war, a rapid development in agriculture took place in Finnmark, with improved lines of communication and an expanded educational system. The little wooden houses and turf huts were destroyed during the war, and were replaced by modern houses and out-buildings. The official support given to the cultivation of the land led to an increase in the areas cultivated. At the same time, the agricultural sector became mechanized, and mowing-machines and tractors are now a common sight in workaday Lapland. The erection of dairies in the coastal areas was an innovation of great significance for the Lapps. The extended network of roads enabled them to market their milk und milk-produce at these dairies. Karasjok, for example, can now sell its milk at a large dairy in Kistrand, a fact which has led to a considerable increase in the milk production.

For the most part, the river Lapps still speak the Lapp language, but the change to Norwegian is taking place here much more rapidly than in the case of the nomadic Lapps. The progressive adaptation to the Norwegian way of life is particularly evident in the large Lapp centres of Karasjok and Kautokeino. The educational system, the church, and local government all show marked Norwegian characteristics. The number of Norwegian newcomers to these Lapp communities is increasing, and the flow of tourists becomes greater year by year. Nevertheless, in spite of these modern influences, the foreign visitor will still find traces of the old Lapp culture in many regions. The Lapp national costume remains a characteristic feature and is worn especially by older people. Good examples of articles made in the traditional Lapp forms are displayed in the shops and demonstrate the Lapps' great skill in handicrafts. The feeling of their common origin has not been quite lost by the river Lapps and the nomadic Lapps. Many river Lapps farm their reindeer out with the nomadic

Lapps in return for the payment of a yearly fee for their supervision. But the adaptation of the sedentary river Lapps to the Norwegian way of life is becoming increasingly apparent.

The Sea Lapps

What has been said concerning the assimilation of the river Lapps with the Norwegian way of life applies even more to the sea Lapps. In many places they have forsaken their own language and the Lapp costume. In almost all domains they have adopted the Norwegian way of living. The Lapp tradition has, of course, been retained in some of the remote fjords; but in these regions, too, the old traditions will disappear when the road system releases the inhabitants from their isolation.

The chief occupations of the sea Lapps are fishing, and, to a lesser extent, agriculture. The sea Lapps were formerly semi-nomadic, and their sources of income were more varied than those of their Norwegian neighbours, who lived mainly by fishing. While the Norwegians usually settled at the mouths of fjords and on islands, the Lapps inhabited the inner regions of the fjords and owned small herds of reindeer. During the 18th century, profitable trucking, i.e. a system of barter, developed between the sea Lapps and Russian skippers bringing merchandise from the White Sea region. This form of trade continued until the outbreak of the Russian Revolution in the year 1917. As a result of this sudden severing of trade relations, the sea Lapps found themselves in a difficult position. With no resources at their disposal, they were confronted with severe competition from Norwegian professional fishermen. For the sea Lapp population, this period of transition was hard and full of privation, and in many places on the coast the development of a Lapp proletariat could be observed. During this time, the assimilation of the sea Lapps with the Norwegians and their adoption of the Norwegian way of life took place all the more rapidly since they had virtually no source of income if they did not know the Norwegian language. Today, the sea Lapp population has recovered from this period of bitter trial and tribulation and, to a great extent, they already own modern fishing equipment. Agriculture also benefited greatly from mechanization, and today it is the main source of income in some areas. Many of the young sea Lapps are engaged in forestry and in maritime commerce.

Origin and Language

After this survey of the Norwegian Lapp groups, let us briefly examine their history. The questions concerning their origin, their race, and their linguistic connections are not all easy to answer, since they are still the subject of scientific controversy. The Lapp's physical structure has characteristic racial features, most evident in the shape of the skull and the exceptionally small stature. His blood also belongs to a special group. Explanations for these physiological characteristics have been sought by various means. According to one theory, the Lapps are a direct off-shoot of the branch from which the white and the yellow races originally sprang; according to another, there is a connection between the small physical stature and Lapland's severe climatic conditions and the prolonged isolation of the Lapps from the outside world. Some of the advocates of the latter theory see in the Lapps the descendants of the bearers of an Arctic culture dating back to the last Ice Age. On account of anthropological similarities between some of the Lapps and the Samoyeds, they have also been regarded as a western group of this people. Differences in the physical build of various Lapp groups have recently given rise to the theory that the Lapp race may be the product of the fusion of two different ethnic groups. Apparently these problems still await elucidation. Examinations of blood-groups recently carried out do not, however, point to any relationship between the Lapps and the Mongolians.

Opinions differ less concerning the earlier dwelling-places and the Lapp culture. As regards the Lapp language, more precise statements are permissible. The language of Lapland belongs to the Finno-Ugric group of languages, two of the best-known of which are Balto-Finnish and Hungarian. Furthermore, the languages of eastern and northern European Russia, as well as the Finno-Ugric languages spoken by the Ostyak and Vogul peoples of north-western Siberia, also belong to this group. Most closely related to the Lapp language is Balto-Finnish; these two language-groups reveal a common origin. The Finno-Ugric group of languages, in turn, is related to the Samoyedic tongues, all of which together form the even larger unit of the Uralian languages. As the build of the Lapps and the Finns differs so greatly, it has been assumed that the Lapps exchanged their own language at an early date for that of the Finns; words are also found which are common to both the Lapp and the Samoyedic languages, but which exist nowhere else. The theory that this proto-Lapp language is a Samoyedic one, however, remains unproved. The fact remains that the Lapps lived in close contact with the ancestors of the Baltic Finns during early primitive Finnish times. In the course of their wanderings west of the Volga region, the Finns reached the Baltic towards the end of the Bronze Age. Here, they met the ancestors of the Lithuanians and the Letts, and borrowed a number of words from them, which the Lapps, in their turn, took over from the Finns. The Lapp form of these words points to their having been adopted in very early Finnish times. Hence the Lapps must have lived in the regions of the inner Baltic and Lake Ladoga, that is, comparatively far south, during that epoch.

At what period the Lapps came to Scandinavia cannot be determined with any certainty, as the linguistic foundations are lacking. However, genuine Lapp designations of species of seals have led to the assumption that the Lapp settlement near the Polar Sea is very old. Archaeological finds on the coasts of Finnmark and Kola, which date from the Bronze Age, are also attributed to the Lapps.

The southern limits of the enormous area over which the Lapps spread during the Bronze Age later moved further and further northwards. This is largely explained by the expansion to the north of the Baltic Finns. It would seem that, already prior to the time of the Vikings, the Lapps had disappeared from south-west Finland. On Lake Ladoga, they were to be found until the 14th century, while they still had settlements in the southern part of eastern Finland in the 17th century. At the beginning of the 19th century, the Lapps were finally forced back to northern Finland. It is quite probable that Lapps also lived in southern Norway in prehistoric times. The place-names indicate that the Lapps had reached Beieren, in Nordland, prior to the time of the Vikings. In historic times, they pressed farther southwards and, before the end of the Middle Ages, the Lapps had probably reached certain areas of Namdalen. In the year 1632 they were also mentioned in South Tröndelag and, only slightly later, in the present-day province of Hedmark. This corresponds roughly to the distribution of the Lapps in Norway today.

Traditional Occupations, Domestic Animals, and Boat-Building

The Lapps of the Bronze Age were a people of hunters and fishers, as is apparent from the Lapp vocabulary. All the old words that denote agriculture and the keeping of domestic animals are of Norse origin. Together with other words, they were assimilated into the Lapp language when the Lapps encountered a country people of northern Norway. Many words with hunting and fishing connotations are, on the other hand, old Lapp, such as the designations for bow, arrow, spear, noose, lasso, and harpoon. The boat, too, has an old Lapp name, likewise the dog, which was originally the Lapps' only domestic animal. The creature most pursued by the old hunter Lapps was the wild reindeer. Reindeer-hunting is a very old art, as is illustrated by the fact that the Lapp and Samoyed methods of capture are practically the same.

The famous archaeological find at Kjelmöya in southern Varanger enable us to trace the history of the Lapps in these parts right back to approximately 400 A.D. These excavations produced a large assortment of implements and the bones of captured animals. The implements were all made of bone, with the exception of a few that were made of iron; none were of stone. Numerous fish-hooks of various types, net-sinkers and netting-needles give indications of the fishing activities of the time. There were also harpoons for catching sea-mammals, above all, probably, the seal. Judging from the fish-spears, the Lapps caught salmon in the rivers. In addition to these articles, arrow-heads, knife-handles, chisels, and the remains of fired clay vessels were discovered. The remains of meals consisted of the bones of fish, birds, and seals, part of a walrus-tusk, and fragments of the rib of a large whale. The bones of reindeer, beaver, fox, wood-marten, and otter were also found. To all appearances, Kjelmöya was a seasonal hunting-ground for semi-nomadic hunters and fishers. They alternated between fishing and hunting at sea, and hunting on the mainland. The sea Lapps in Finnmark were semi-nomadic until last century.

During their progress southwards along the Norwegian coast, the Lapps met Scandinavian farmers. They adopted these people's simple agricultural implements, as well as their domestic animals, including even the cat. This contact must have taken place prior to the Viking era, in primitive Nordic times. The spread of agriculture and the keeping of domestic animals in the Lapp area along the coast as far as Varanger is due to the contact of the Lapps with Scandinavians. These influences did not penetrate as far as Kola, for the connections between the Lapps of the peninsula and those of Varanger were not close. These first meetings between farmers of northern Norway and Lapps probably took place in the Senja-Ofoten-Tysfjord area, and it may be assumed that the Lapps were also fluent in the language of their northern Scandinavian neighbours. The Norwegians also instructed the Lapps in the construction of new types of boats. In those days the Lapps appear to have used canoe-type boats made of skins and propelled by means of a paddle, but words borrowed from the Norse boat-terminology seem to indicate that the Lapps also learnt to build wooden boats. This knowledge of boat-building was of the utmost economic significance to the Lapps who inhabited the densely-wooded regions on the upper reaches of the fjords. They became outstanding boat-builders, and for many centuries they supplied the whole of northern Norway with vessels. Thus, a cultural difference developed between these Lapps and those of the north, who remained semi-nomadic hunters and fishers for a much longer period.

The Taxation of the Lapps

In early times, the Lapps were dependent on their Nordic neighbours, who were better armed and better organized. When their neighbours secured for themselves the right of supervision over the Lapp people, their main motive was of an economic nature. The Lapps were well known as skilled hunters, and they lived in areas teeming with fur-bearing animals. Furs were already highly valued as merchandise in prehistoric times. As archaeological finds indicate, a fur trade probably existed between Lapps, Finns, and Scandinavians already in the Bronze Age. It was this trade that subsequently gave rise to the levying of taxes on the Lapps. Tax-collectors divided the Lapp country among themselves and levied taxes in kind, the medium being furs.

This so-called Finn-tax was soon extended, in northern Norway, to other commodities. An old literary source gives us a survey of the taxes paid by the Lapps during the Viking era.

We find this survey in a report which the maritime explorer Ohthere made for King Alfred of England at the end of the 9th century. According to Ohthere, he lived farthest north of any Norwegian. On the occasion of an expedition to Finnmark and the Kola peninsula, he had found this region to be uninhabited, with the exception of a few Lapp fishermen, bird-catchers, and hunters. Furthermore, he is alleged to have possessed 600 'tame, unbought' reindeer; six of these animals were decoys, which rated high in Lapp favour, owing to their importance in the capture of wild reindeer. It appears from Ohthere's description that his main source of wealth was the taxes paid by the Lapp people. These consisted chiefly of furs, birds' feathers, walrus-tusks and tow-ropes, which were made from the skins of whales and seals. Each Lapp paid according to his social position. Wealthy Lapps were generally taxed at the rate of 15 marten skins, 5 reindeer, 1 bear pelt, 10 buckets of feathers, 1 coat of bearskin and 1 of otter skin, as well as two tow-ropes, each 60 ells in length.

Ohthere's document contains many indications concerning the Lapps' way of life and their relations with the farmers of northern Norway during the time of the Vikings. Those Lapps who lived in the vicinity of Ohthere's settlement were directly under his supervision and had to pay him tribute. Ohthere presumably lived to the north of the region which was the old Lapp agricultural centre. Even if they kept tame reindeer, they lived chiefly by fishing and by bear, whale and seal hunting. Concerning the northern Lapps, Ohthere relates that they hunted in winter and engaged in deep-sea fishing in summer. Like the Kjelmöya Lapps, they were thus semi-nomadic. Since payment of taxes by Ohthere himself to the King are not mentioned, it may be assumed that he paid none.

The taxation of the Lapps by the Crown, perhaps at the time of Harald Haarfager (Harold Fairhair), changed all this. Egil's saga tells of a northern Norwegian chieftain of those days who served as the King's tax-collector. He lived at Vefsn, and his name was Thorolf Kveldulvsson. With a retinue of a hundred men, he penetrated far into the present-day Swedish-Lapp area for the purpose of collecting his taxes. The Norwegian kings seem to have extended the taxation of the Lapps right up to Kola even before the 11th century. In Finnmark, the tax-collectors of Norway, Sweden, Finland, and Russia all met, and the area became a bone of contention. As the state-taxation levied on the Lapps increased, it was used more and more by the states concerned as the basis of territorial claims in Lapp regions. In some places, the Lapps had to pay taxes to three different kingdoms simultaneously, because the state frontiers had not yet been marked. Frontiers were settled between Norway and Sweden only in 1751, and between Norway and Russia in the year 1826.

The Social Order and the Family

Under the difficult circumstances of their lives, the Lapps never succeeded in founding a state of their own. Reports from old sources tell of Lapp kings, but it is doubtful whether such kings ever really existed. In spite of the pressure brought to bear on them by their neighbours, the Lapps succeeded in creating a remarkable form of social order: the Lapp village, or *siida*. Relics of this institution still exist among the nomadic Lapps. It is, however, older than the breeding of reindeer and dates back to the time of the purely hunting and fishing culture. Originally, the *siida* comprised a group of hunters and fishers who shared rights over a common area. At the same time, they promoted co-operation within the community, and protected hunting-grounds and fishing-grounds from over-exploitation. The organization of the *siida* was also in the interests of the tax-collectors and traders; it was permitted to carry out its functions as long as it proved to be in no way detrimental to the incipient colonization. In the case of Russia's Skolt Lapps, interesting forms of the *siida* have been preserved until recent times. Thus, in the Petsamo region, the Lapp population was divided into three *siidas,* each connected with certain water-courses. The 'executive committee' of the *siida,* comprising a member of every family belonging to it, made decisions concerning the acceptance of new members, and protected the interests of the *siida* in matters involving its neighbours. This authoritative body also shared out land to the families and could undertake the re-distribution of fishing-grounds, even though these were as a rule hereditary. The hunting of wild reindeer was the communal concern of the *siida,* while each individual family was free to hunt small game on the hunting-ground allotted to it. The 'executive committee' of the *siida* took legal decisions in lesser criminal cases and was competent for the marking of the reindeer. The *siida,* as a community, cared for the sick and the aged. In some details, the functions of a non-Russian *siida* may have differed from those of the Skolt Lapps, but many common characteristics indicate the long history of these Lapp communities. Big game hunting, for example, was the prerogative of the *siida* assembly in all regions, as was the allotting of hunting-grounds and fishing-grounds. A spirit of mutual consideration reigned everywhere; nobody within the *siida* was allowed to suffer privation, and goods were equitably shared. Anyone who lacked the bare necessities was entitled to claim assistance from the others.

According to an unwritten law, hunting was for the men, while it was the women's task to prepare the skins and make clothes. By reason of an old Lapp tradition and certain hunting taboos, the meat of freshly-slaughtered reindeer was cooked by the men. The women, however, participated in fishing and took their turn in watching over the herds; and while it was the man who looked after the reindeer trade, he always considered the advice of his wife. The woman is held in esteem in the Lapp family and she is independent. She is also usually consulted in matters of finance. The relationship between parents and children is harmonious; in fact, Lapp children are seldom smacked.

The old Lapp customs regarding betrothal and marriage were based on economic considerations, which still play a certain rôle, though not a decisive one. The suitor had to offer gifts to the parents and relatives of his prospective bride. Originally, these gifts were actually payment for the bride. The acceptance or rejection of the bridegroom was left largely to the discretion of the bride's mother.

The courtship took place in a festive setting, and certain ceremonial forms have been retained until the present day. On his journey to the girl's home, the bridegroom took with him several 'spokesmen', who were to speak in his favour on his visit to the bride's parents. There were often lively debates between the two parties, each striving to present the qualities of the prospective partner in as favourable a light as possible. The bride's parents tried to obtain the best possible material settlement. In olden days, part of the bride's 'purchase price' consisted of the bridegroom's undertaking to live with his parents-in-law for a certain length of time after the marriage and to work for them. In even more distant times, the Lapps probably regulated the choice of partners according to a complicated system of relationships based on kinship and age-group.

If we sometimes find it difficult to comprehend the reactions of the Lapps, the reason frequently lies in their specific conceptions of justice, or in their ancient traditions. If, for example, the nomadic Lapps consider the theft of a reindeer less serious than other crimes, it is because formerly the reindeer, being a half-wild animal, did not represent personal property. The Lapps also have their own conception of the rights of succession; while, in the case of the Norwegians, the eldest son is the chief heir, this privilege falls to the youngest according to Lapp law.

Lapp Dwellings and Costumes

Besides the tent of the nomadic Lapps, which we already know, the turf-covered 'earth-huts' of the Lapps also deserve brief mention. In the olden days, they were the usual dwelling-places of the sedentary Lapps, particularly of those in the coastal areas. The nomadic Lapps also owned turf-huts on their summer pastures, and we also find such huts near the fishing-grounds in the interior of the country. The framework of the turf-huts is of wood overlaid with bark, and the outside is covered with sods right up to the roof. As in the case of the tent, we also find two main types of wooden structure. Instead of tentpoles, wooden posts or boards are set up close together. According to the type of construction, the result was either a dome-shaped or a conical turf-hut. The so-called Norwegian hut, a third type, is still occasionally built. It is a house of normal shape in Norwegian style, with perpendicular walls and rafters; the turf-covered, sloping roof is almost pyramid-shaped.

In the coastal tracts, we find all the various hut forms. The most primitive type of dwelling was the 'common hut', where man and beast lodged together; the hygienic conditions naturally left much to be desired. The three-part hut was more satisfactory, with its common entrance and separate accommodation for the family and the animals on either side of a passage. These Lapp houses could be enlarged with annexes. Life is more comfortable in the turf-huts than in the tent; variations in temperature are offset by the walls. The turf-hut is presumably older than the tent, and probably served as a pattern for the latter. Since early times, the Lapps have also lived in timber-built houses. In the coastal regions they adopted this type of construction from the

Norwegians, and in the interior of Finnmark probably from the Finns who settled there at the beginning of the 18th century. The turf-hut had always been popular with the Lapps, mainly because it was easy to build, requiring only turf and simple pieces of wood for its construction. In the sparsely-wooded parts of the country, the Lapps adapted their homes to their natural surroundings. The Lapp costume, too, is well adapted to Nature. The winter clothes afford excellent protection against the cold. The outer coat, trousers, and footwear are of reindeer skin, worn hair outwards. Underclothing is mainly of cloth fabric. In the old days, the Lapps wore an inner garment made of supple reindeer-calf skin or sheepskin. They put hay in their pliable skin shoes in order to absorb the moisture and assure an even temperature. Both winter and summer shoes have upward-pointing toes. When the Lapp is ski-ing, the point of the winter shoe lies under the toe-straps of the skis and prevents them from slipping off. Tanned leather is used for the summer costume.

The summer coat, in recent times worn only in Tysfjord, was also made of leather. Nowadays, fabrics are preferred to leather for the summer coats: coarse woollen material is used for everyday wear and cloth for best. The man's coat is shorter than that of the woman and, in contrast to the latter, has a high collar. The neckline of the man's coat is I-shaped, while that of the woman's is Y- or V-shaped. Before modern underwear became an everyday possession in Lapland, the throat was covered with a so-called 'breast cloth' attached round the neck. In the case of the Lapps in the more southerly parts of the country, it was decorated with multi-coloured pewter-thread embroidery. Here, the men wear the summer coat open at the front in the same way as the winter coat. Summer and winter coats are held in place by a belt.

Today, the men prefer wide leather belts, and the women have belts made of cloth or woollen yarn woven or plaited into attractive designs and patterns. The men's leather belts are sometimes adorned with little metal plates or shoe-eyelets. The man wears his knife in his belt, while the woman often has a little bag containing sewing-requisites suspended from it. The man's coat is pulled up over the belt, thus forming a make-shift pocket, in which pipe and tobacco pouch can be kept. The Lapps make sure that the belts sits properly so that the coat may be shown off to its best advantage. Young girls, above all, like the coat to 'flap out' well and truly behind them and, to this end, frequently wear more than one at a time. The Lapp coat has ornamental bands of various colours stitched on to it. Formerly, these coats were always unicoloured and this is still the case in Karasjok today. In Kautokeino, however, people later adopted bands with floral and other *motifs,* which cover a large part of the back.

Waterproof footwear is indispensable in summer and, for this reason, the tanned leather shoes are rubbed with tar and grease. Wearing leather trousers, the Lapps are able to wade through swamps and rivers without getting wet. Headwear differs from one region to another, and is an indication of where the Lapp comes from. In Finnmark, the man's cap is star-shaped and has four points; the woman's cap is close-fitting at the front and pocket-shaped at the back, with ear-flaps at the sides. In the south, both men and women wear a high pointed cap, which is nearly always trimmed with pewter-thread embroidery. As we have seen, the Lapp costume has already disappeared in many places, above all in the coastal regions, where assimilation with the Norwegian way of life is most advanced. In other places, it is now worn as a festive costume, and its continued existence is therefore assured. The nomadic Lapps are unlikely to give up their winter costume as, in extreme cold, it is superior to all other types of clothing.

Religious Conceptions and Practices

The old Lapps' conception of life was based on the fundamental idea that all things are controlled by nature-spirits. According to their belief, these 'powers' of Nature were either well-disposed or ill-disposed, depending on a man's behaviour. These powers determined the destiny of men and the course of the world. The Lapp ancestors played an important rôle among the powers. According to Lapp belief, they dwelt in certain mountains, which were revered by the families and inherited rather like worldly goods, thus remaining in the family. The heavenly bodies and the elements were also venerated. The daily cult was directed towards so-called *sieides,* that is, stones or other things in Nature whose singular shapes attracted attention. The Lapp people attributed special power to these objects, to which they made sacrifices in order to assure themselves good fortune while hunting and fishing. While each family worshipped its own 'cult objects', the *siida* had, as a common sanctuary, a *sieide* which was larger than all the others and of much greater importance. The bear cult, which was common throughout the Arctic regions, was practised by the entire Lapp village. The veneration of the bear was based on the notion of the particular cunning and the dangerous nature of an animal that can walk upright, thus resembling human beings. According to an old Lapp belief, the *noaides,* who were able to establish contact with the other world when in ecstasy, were mediators between man and the invisible powers. This form of belief is prevalent in the Arctic and sub-Arctic regions of the northern hemisphere; it is also called Shamanism, from the Siberian word *shaman* for *noaide.* The most important instrument of the *shamans* and *noaides* was the drum. When, for example, some grave illness necessitated the invocation of the powers, the people gathered round the *noaide,* who beat the drum until he fell into a trance. This was the moment when the *noaide's* soul left his body and went to the other world in order to fetch help and advice. He was accompanied on this dangerous journey by assistant spirits. When Shamanism declined, the drum became a soothsaying instrument. Symbolic figures were painted on the drum-skin, and a piece of metal was placed on it; the prophecy depended on the figure upon which the metal came to rest when the drum was beaten. These ecstatic phenomena had a strong influence on the Lapps' neighbours and many fantastic reports exist concerning bilocation, the Lapps' ability to be in two different places at the same time. They were spoken of as if they were dangerous sorcerers and the most peculiar ideas sprang up concerning their magic powers. However, these notions brought with them certain advantages for the Lapps, for newcomers feared to settle in their vicinity.

The Lapps were always ready to accept fresh religious impulses from the religious conceptions of neighbouring peoples, just as they were receptive in other matters, and we also find Christian elements. According to ancient Finno-Russian loan-words, an early Christian influence on the Lapps appears to have come from the east. The earliest mission in Lapland appears to have come from Norway. In the course of the 14th century, one hears of Swedish Lapps being baptized, while it appears that the Russian Lapps were first converted to Christianity during the 16th century. As these conversions apparently took place only sporadically, it would seem that the activities of the missions left no very great impression on the Lapps.

Christianity must have seemed to the Lapps a total renunciation of their own ancient religion, so closely associated with Nature, upon whose laws they all depended. It was only in the 18th century, with the dawn of pietism, that intensive missionary activity commenced. The Norwegian pastor Thomas von Westen, who is also called the Apostle of the Lapps, was a pioneer in this field. In the same century the Swedes, fired by the Norwegian's activities, followed his example. About the middle of the

19th century, Laestadianism, a strange new religious awakening, began to spread. This religious movement was named after the Swedish pastor, Lars Levi Laestadius, one of the most remarkable figures in the history of the Nordic Church. Of Swedish-Lapp origin, he was born at Arjeplog in about 1800. He grew up in poverty and in unfavourable circumstances, and became a pastor in 1825, devoting himself throughout his life to religious works in the Finno-Lapp regions of northernmost Sweden. The social and cultural conditions in Lapland at that time were bad. Alcoholism was rife among the population and hindered favourable development. Laestadius took up the cudgels against spirits, but the fight was long and arduous. In the year 1844, Laestadius experienced a new spiritual upsurge; his preaching became so inspiring that the religious revival spread to Norway and Finland. This movement had a most beneficial effect on the Lapps, whose self-confidence was strengthened, for it was often Lapps who took over the leadership of Laestadian groups, even in communities with many Norwegian members. Today, the Laestadians are split up into various camps which attack one another bitterly.

Like the earlier Lapp Shamanism, Laestadianism also bears distinctly ecstatic characteristics. Religious meetings often end with the assembled company embracing each other and promising mutual forgiveness of their sins. In many respects, this sect adopts a depreciatory attitude towards modern culture, thus favouring the preservation of the traditional Lapp way of life. On the other hand, its condemnation of certain 'worldly' manifestations has a culturally impoverishing influence. Thus, for instance, the Lapp 'horn cap' met with disapproval on the grounds that it was 'the seat of the devil of vanity'. The strictest form of Laestadianism regards every representation of man and beast as sinful. The traditional Lapp singing is also regarded as condemnable, because the texts of the songs are thought to be too 'worldly'.

Art and Ornament

The Lapps are an alert and lively people. They have a pronounced aptitude for the art of ornamentation, which is shown to advantage on their wooden and horn articles, and in textiles. As the adornment of the national costume proves, they also have a well-developed sense of colour. In older times, the Lapps used to paint primitive symbolic figures on the 'magic' drum. These were executed in a red pigment extracted from chewed alder-bark. Among the *motifs* were the Lapp village, Lapp occupations, Nature and religion, reindeer, elks, bears, beavers, wild birds and fish. The sun-god, wind-god, and thunder-god, and other mythological figures were also depicted. The demon of disease appeared in the form of a horseman, suggestive of the Teutonic god, Odin. Christian *motifs,* such as Christ, Mary, the Apostles, and churches, are also found. The interpretation is partly stylised, partly naturalistic.

Their figurative art is sometimes compared with the ancient cave-paintings in more southerly regions, and with the rock-engravings of the north, which tend mainly towards the magical. With the missionaries' condemnation of Shamanism and the burning of the 'magic' drum, the painting tradition was also abandoned, in so far as it was the expression of these practices. During the time of the shamans, pieces of blunt horn and wood served the artists as utensils; today they naturally have brushes and a wide range of colours at their disposal. The life and natural surroundings of the reindeer Lapps are often found as *motifs*.

Of the modern Lapp artists, John Savio of Finnmark and Nils Skum of Sweden should be mentioned. Savio, who died young, studied at the Academy of Art in Oslo. In addition to painting, he practised wood-carving with eminent skill. His pictures were striking characterizations of his models—the Lapp, reindeer, dog, and wolf. Nils Skum was a 'primitive' artist, who enjoyed no academic training. His main themes were reindeer and mountains, and he created pictures of a fascinating beauty with the simplest of means. His portrayal of large reindeer herds is unequalled.

Lapp ornamentation has been influenced from many quarters, but it nevertheless retains its Lapp imprint. The rendering of details varied according to the region and there were qualitative differences; the best work, however, achieves a remarkably high standard. The Lapps of the north were distinguished particularly for the beauty of their plaited and woven decorations, and those of the south attained considerable skill in decorative handicrafts executed in wood, horn, and bone. Lapp ornamentation is mainly geometrical. In the case of wooden and horn objects, the decoration consists of dots, triangles, and circles, as well as lines, and it is carved with a knife. Naturalistic representations of man and beast are also to be found. The manual skill of the northern Lapps was inferior to that of their southern compatriots, and was more effective when seen from a distance, while the minute work of the latter was enchanting and the detail subtly wrought.

The Lapps in southern regions possessed special dexterity in pewter-thread embroidery, in imitation of the gold-thread and silver-thread embroidery of their Scandinavian neighbours. The procedure consists in drawing a thin strip of pewter through a series of holes, each smaller than the last, until it takes on the appearance of thread. The pewter-thread is then spun round a length of sewing-thread or a sinew, whereupon attractive designs are stitched on to material and skins. Basket-making, an art which was very widespread in Lapland in earlier times, has now practically died out.

Music, Folklore, and Poetry

Astonishing as it may seem, the Lapps have never possessed a national musical instrument, with the exception of the drum and a form of 'flute' or pipe made from hollow plant-stems. The music of the Lapps was singing. Apparently their old songs often had a religious or magical theme. The Lapp language does not actually know a word for 'song' in the sense of a sung poem, although various expressions for 'singing' exist, such as the Finnish loan-word *law'lot.*

In Norwegian and Swedish, Lapp singing is denoted by the word *joik* (pronounced *yoike*), a derivation from the old Lapp *juoigat* meaning 'sing'.

Lapp songs differ from the Scandinavian and other European folk-songs, but have much in common with those of the Ostyaks, the Voguls, and the Samoyeds. The origin of the *joik* goes back to the days of early antiquity; the predominant characteristics are rhythm and melody. Expletives such as 'la-la', 'valla', 'lo-lo', and 'na-na' are frequently found. In Pite Lappmark, certain songs consist entirely of such syllables; they are sung, for example, by the herdsmen to calm the reindeer and keep away the wolves. Many of the *joiks* have an onomatopœic, or imitative, character, human speech, animal noises, the soughing of the wind, and the bluster of the storm being represented by the rhythm and the melodic line. This main theme is often accompanied by a short set of words, which are repeated *ad libitum.* In Finnmark, for example, it is this type of song which predominates. The words of Lapp songs are often satirical, referring to unfortunate, grotesque, or sometimes even erotic episodes in the life of a person. Those sung about are also often typified by such phrases as 'with the smile of an angel but the nature of a fox'. Short improvised *joiks* are often emotional descriptions of a certain atmosphere or mood. The reindeer herdsman may burst spontaneously into song at the sight of his herd or of a green pasture. In Norway, epic *joiks* are sung, especially in Varanger. In comparison with the spontaneous *joiks,* however, they are often rather prosaic.

The contents of the *joiks* vary greatly. Remnants of the Shamanistic beliefs are rare, and the names of the old gods have disappeared, but the *noaides* feature in several of them. Thus, one *joik* recalls how two of these *noaides* tried to shift the position of some islands: 'Varanger Island, go over there! Aina Island, come over here!' Yet another *joik motif* concerns the wolf, of whom it is said, 'The wolf, ah yes, the wolf, ho-ho-ho / through nine valleys at dusk / he runs, runs, runs'. Whole districts may be characterized in a *joik*. A Finnmark *joik* confers upon Kautokeino the nickname of 'blood knife', as a reminder of the killing of two people during the religious disturbances in that village in the year 1852. Karasjok is called 'magnificent horn', Polmak 'horn of the law', and Utsjok 'worn-out fur'. Lengthy songs with a purely lyrical content are rare. Two of these, however, first drew attention to the artistic value of Lapp songs; they were published in 1673 by Johannes Schefferus in 'Lapponia', the first monograph on Lapland. Both these songs depict the yearning of a Lapp youth for his beloved. Adapted by Herder, Kleist, and Longfellow, these songs have found their way into world literature.

The Lapps possess a rich store of legends and fairy-tales, the dividing line between these two traditional forms often being difficult to draw. J. Qvigstad has divided them into the following groups: animal fables, fairy-stories with supernatural *motifs*, fairy-stories of the stupid giant, and comic tales. In the animal fables, the bear, the wolf, and the fox are predominant; the reindeer is seldom mentioned. All the groups include many *motifs* that are common to many peoples and, unlike the *joiks*, do not depict distinctive Lapp surroundings and conceptions. A favourite fairy-tale theme is the outwitting of the stupid giant, Stallo, by the Lapps. In one of these stories we find the Polyphemus *motif*.

The humorous fairy-story appears in the tale of the man with the quarrelsome wife, whom he pushes into a deep hole in the ground. After a few days, however, he begins to feel bored and throws a long rope down the hole. When it is grasped at the other end, the man pulls on the rope, only to find that he has hauled up the Devil, who explains that he is unable to endure the wicked woman any longer. The legends actually give a better idea of Lapp tradition. Here, too, we meet Stallo, the giant, the Lapps' adversary. When he challenges a Lapp to a wrestling match, his appearance is heralded by a whistling sound. In the folklore of the Samoyeds, the approach of a similar monster is also accompanied by this whistling. An interesting feature of several legends is the identification of Stallo with the moon, which descends to earth in order to devour disobedient children. Numerous legends deal with the severe taxation of the Lapps by neighbouring countries, stress being laid on the cunning by which the Lapps evaded their tormentors. Lapp heroes, such as Baeive-Olav and Laurukash, also overcome their opponents in open combat. In Lapp legends, mention is often made of the Chudes, presumably a Finnish tribe, who demanded high taxes and exploited the Lapps. In order to keep these Chudes away, the Lapps built themselves underground homes. In one story, the attention of a Chude is drawn to these secret dwellings by the crying of a baby. Before going to call his people, the Chude marks the spot with a stick. But the Lapps have been warned and they remove the stick to another place, thus putting the Chudes off the scent. Another widespread legend is that of the Lapp on skis who guides the Chudes over a mountain during the night. He leads the group with a flaming torch, which he suddenly throws into an abyss and then dodges nimbly aside, whereupon the Chudes follow the flare down into the bottom of the gorge.

The *shamans* or *noaides,* with their magic powers, often appear in the legends. Even Stallo was afraid of them, for they were generally victorious in the combat thanks to their powers of sorcery. Occasionally mention is made of the conflict between the Lapp religion and Christianity. Thus, we read of a sacrificial stone which was burnt by Baeive-Olav, who, embittered because it had not helped him while he was out hunting, invoked the Trinity. The stories of the origin of curious freaks of Nature are sometimes amusing. According to one ancient legend, the 'Man in the Moon' was once a thief who had a grudge against the moonlight, because it prevented him from stealing. So he went up to the moon in order to paint it with tar; unfortunately, in his efforts, he got stuck to the tar-bucket. According to other sources, it is not a man at all, but a wicked woman called Atcheshaedne.

One legend relates that the dog, the Lapps' most loyal servant, made a compact with the Lapp people in remote antiquity to serve them in return for payment in the form of broth, bones, and a noose; the old Lapps at that time used to destroy old dogs by hanging them instead of by killing them with a knife. Of the wolf, the reindeer's most inveterate enemy, it is said that he was created by the Devil and placed in God's way. In order to remove the obstacle, God was forced to breathe life into the animal. Riddles were less popular among the Lapps and they are rarely found. Proverbs, on the other hand, are very numerous. The nomadic Lapp says, 'Travel is better than repose'; the Norwegian, on the other hand, 'East or West, Home is best'. According to the Lapps, 'Still water has a lot of sediment', while for the Norwegians 'Still waters run deep'. Lapp literature is of modest proportions. Pedar Jalvi of Utsjok, in the Tana valley, was a talented poet who died young. The poems he wrote were few, but the Lapps have taken them to their hearts. The poem entitled 'Snowflakes' tells of his conviction that the Lapps, as a distinct group, will continue to exist as long as they remain united (free translation of the poem see next page).

Through the air, fine snowflakes float silently down on to the field,
on to stones and birch trees, covering the earth with a blanket of white.

They are only very tiny, but, together, they are millions,
they cover ditches, valleys, trees, forming drifts among the bushes,
and building great glaciers over the rocks.

The warmth of the spring sun melts the little snowflakes,
turning them into clear, pure drops; and the drops reassemble to form
the spring, the river, the lake, the sea. Great is then the strength of the tiny one.

Another Lapp writer was Matti Aikio of Karasjok, who wrote in Norwegian. His novels give a moving description of the loneliness of the Lapps in foreign cultural surroundings.

The Future of the Lapps and of their Culture

If we consider the Lapp people from the point of view of their number, and trace the repeated attempts made by the northern States to assimilate this racial minority culturally, it is astonishing that one can actually still speak of a Lapp culture and a Lapp language. That this is so may be ascribed principally to their ability to adopt elements of foreign languages and culture, and to adapt them to their own linguistic and cultural pattern. We may, with some justification, speak of a 'relict' culture, which has retained elements now forgotten by the peoples from whom they were once borrowed. This Lapp characteristic is the expression of their conservative turn of mind, their mode of life in the isolation of the extreme north also being a co-determinating factor.

Earlier, however, the Lapp culture did not differ from that of neighbouring peoples to such an extent that foreign influences were ever able to cause a real dissolution of the Lapp way of living. Today, one can no longer speak of an actual isolation of the Lapp districts. Modern lines of communication have now opened up these remote territories, and the Lapp educational system has been brought up to date and modelled on the Norwegian system. There is also the assimilating influence of the radio, even if an occasional broadcast is now made in the Lapp language. The monetary system, which has now been generally introduced in Lapland, and the many different aspects of modern competition, have all contributed to the far-reaching disintegration of the Lapp tradition, a fact which is quite obvious today.

The situation in the cultural sphere has undergone radical changes in comparison with earlier times, and it must be admitted that the outlook for the Lapp culture beside that of the modern northern States is not very promising. There is nevertheless much that indicates that the Lapp culture is unlikely to disappear completely in the immediate future. Certain tendencies in cultural policy with regard to Lapland have changed. The pressure exerted towards adaptation in the linguistic domain has been relaxed, and the Lapp language is used as an auxiliary language in the schools in the Lapp regions. School-books are printed in the Lapp language, which has also been introduced at the Teachers' Training College at Tromsö. A new hymn-book for Lapps has been published, and public subsidies have been granted for the promotion of Lapp literature. A significant event was also the establishment of two advisory organs for Lapp affairs: the Nordic Lapp Council and the Lapp Council for Finnmark, the majority of whose members are Lapps.

Many Lapps have lost faith in the value of their culture and desire the speediest and fullest transition to Norwegian. In their opinion, the Lapp language only hinders the learning of Norwegian and makes it difficult to find employment. This attitude is dis-

88 Whaler amid pack-ice at the entrance to Is Fjord during the polar night
89 Drift ice, in the background aerial reflection

puted in both Lapp and Norwegian quarters, where it is argued that nobody can, with impunity, renounce his mother-tongue and reject his own cultural heritage. It is, indeed, the Lapp language which lies at the heart of the entire Lapp question, for upon their mother-tongue alone rests the identity of the Lapps as a distinct national group. If the continuance of the Lapp language is to be assured, it is necessary that a Lapp *élite* should take its promotion to heart and develop it further. One of the pre-requisites is the creation of higher-grade schools, the organization of which shall take Lapp tradition into account. A corner-stone of the foundation has already been laid through the School for Lapp Youth at Karasjok. At Kautokeino, a school of handicrafts has been founded for the promotion of Lapp handwork. The extension of instruction given in the Lapp language at Oslo University, and the granting of scholarships to teachers at Lapp schools for the advanced study of the Lapp language at the academic level should also be mentioned.

It is the youth of today that will ultimately decide the destiny of the Lapp language and the Lapp culture. If they set their hearts on preserving the heritage of their fathers, it will also be possible to speak of Lapps in Norway in the future.

Asbjörn Nesheim

90 Magdalena Bay, on Spitsbergen

91

91 View from Ny-Ålesund across Kongs Fjord

92 Colliery in Ny-Ålesund, on Spitsbergen

93 In summer a tubulent river rushes down the Longyearbyen valley (Spitsbergen). That is why the houses stand on its flanks

94 Reindeer

95

95 Hawk-weed
96 Catchfly
97 Pack-ice piling up into hummocks
98 Foreland hem with beach ridges: Freeman Sound, tongue of Freeman glacier (Spitsbergen)
99 'Marine line' at an altitude of 160 and 250 feet in Neu-Bayerland, Edge Island (Spitsbergen)
100 Heavy pack-ice cover with evidence of strong compression
101 Luxury liners carry an ever increasing flow of tourists to Spitsbergen
102 Cape Linné on Is Fjord
103 A rare sunny day lends the mountains a fairy-tale aspect

97

98

99

Spitsbergen

Far to the north of Norway, midway between the North Cape and the North Pole, lies a group of islands, the ridges and pinnacles of whose mountains are covered with snow and in whose bays, fjords, and valleys a fascinating wealth of colour and an astonishingly abundant flora enjoys a brief Arctic summer: Spitsbergen—alpine land in the Arctic Ocean, the island of everlasting sunshine in summer and of black polar night in winter; Svalbard—land of the cool coasts. Four large islands and a number of small ones form a closely-knit group of quite peculiar charm, upon which—stamped as they are by the juncture of the outermost waters of the Gulf Stream and the compact all-year polar ice—both arctic cold and oceanic moderation are found.

When one catches sight for the first time of Svalbard's foothills, after a journey over thousands of kilometres of Arctic Ocean, one enters upon a veritable wonderland: in a region where trees have little chance to grow and where the vegetation can never be dense, an unexpected wealth of flora unfolds for a brief, three-month period of efflorescence. One hundred and fifty different species of plants in the gayest colours grow in the more sheltered places, among them lichens and mosses, as well as tough grasses and moisture-loving reeds, and also a truly amazing number of flowers. However far apart the individual flowers may grow, it is thanks to them that a green shimmer nevertheless covers the mountain slopes far to the north on the main island. Above it, the white of 'firn' and glacier, and below, in sharp contrast, the waters of the bay, at times cool and greeny-blue, at others a rich, deep shade of sapphire. Over all this beauty gleams an azure sky, and that silver sheen peculiar to the Arctic radiates across the entire countryside—a sheen which turns not only the great expanse of the open sea to silver, but also the gold of the sun. For Central Europeans the most amazing thing is doubtless the fact that during four whole months—from mid-April to mid-August—it never grows dark in the Far North. The sun, however low it may circle the sky, does not actually set, with the result that it is difficult to tell the time of day by its position. How easy it is to forget the regularity of the common round: here one eats when one is hungry and sleeps when one feels tired.

In winter, however, it is the other way round. The sun is not seen even once for three-and-a-half months; the island waits in the cold and desolation of the polar night for the first ray of sunshine, the first revitalizing warmth—though no one goes to Spitsbergen in winter. Cut off from the outside world, the archipelago is entrenched behind the pack-ice, which prevents the entry of all shipping. An omnipresent blanket of snow and, above it, a similar covering of clouds also make air-communication impossible. It is quiet and lonely on Spitsbergen at that season. One yearns for the long summer days when the June sun melts the snow and the ice breaks up, and when the vegetation re-appears almost overnight.

Two Discoveries—Two Names

The Vikings called it 'Svalbard', this island hidden right up in the north; it must already have been discovered by them a thousand years ago. They sailed round the North Cape as early as the year 890 and penetrated to Iceland and Greenland during the century that followed. It is certain that the name 'Svalbard' first appeared in that Icelandic 'colonization report' (landnamabok) which is an invaluable source for the history of the discovery and colonization of the north.

The name Spitsbergen dates back to the re-discovery of the island—which had meanwhile sunk into oblivion again—by the Dutchmen Willem Barents and Cornelius Rijp, who, instead of finding what they were actually looking for—a north-east passage for more convenient maritime traffic with the Far East—found an island with many pointed mountains on its west coast. Because 'pointed mountains' were 'spitsbergen' in their language, the island got the name it bears today. This can only possibly apply to the north-west corner of the main island, western Spitsbergen, which is the only one to answer to this description within a wide circle ranging from Iceland over Jan Mayen and Bear Island to Franz Josef Island and Novaya Zemlya. Instead of the wealth of India and China, the Dutchmen brought home news of the whale and the seal. It was soon to be proved just how excellent were the possibilities of economic exploitation afforded by this region in the Far North.

Forms and Formations

When Barents re-discovered the island in 1596, he called the island 'Spitsbergen' and introduced an era of systematic exploitation and exploration of the Arctic. Once having seen Spitsbergen from Kreuzfjord or Magdalena Bay, no one can deny the justification of this designation. Here in the north, the country is indeed full of pointed peaks, an alpine land in the Arctic Ocean. The comparison with the ridges and peaks of the Aare Massif or the Mont Blanc region constantly suggests itself. This is hardly surprising, for the rock substratum is the same in both regions: gneisses and granites of the original rock crust of our planet—pressed up in the Alps by Tertiary tectonic faulting, pushed up as a result of older tectonic faulting slightly higher in northern Spitsbergen than in the southern half of the island. There, in the south, numerous strata were deposited during the Palaeozoic and Mesozoic over the Archaean (Pre-Cambrian) crust of the earth: Silurian, Devonian, and Carboniferous strata below, and on these Trias, Jurassic, and Lower Cretaceous strata, with Tertiary sandstones, marls, and calcareous deposits above these. Flat stratification here results in flat-topped mountains, wide ridges, and broad plateaux, which descend abruptly into valleys deeply eroded by water and, above all, by ice. Where these two worlds—the pointed and the broad-ridged 'spitsbergen'—meet, singular contrasts dominate the scene. The deepest fjord in the island is Is Fjord, along this tectonic fracture on its northern shore (a 'fault' in the language of the geologist), a landscape in which sharply-defined mountain chains of dark old rock alternate with broad glacial valleys, most of which continue down to the coast, where they end in a steep drop: an alpine range that has been plunged 3,000 metres (9,840 feet) into the ocean. On the southern side, where lie the well-known Green Harbour and Advent Bay, there is a grey-brown and grey-violet world of steep scree-covered slopes, with broad valleys containing numerous chains of lakes below, an amazing thickness of flat-lying strata above them, and wide flat-topped ridges, often covered with 'firn' and 'icecakes', higher still. Towards the eastern edge of the main island and on the neighbouring island to the east, the 'firn' covering is compacted to form real inland ice.

Thus Spitsbergen has three faces: an Arctic one, with this inland ice in the east and in the interior of the northern part of the island, a circumglacial one, lying clear of this present-day ice covering, in the flat south, and an Alpine face in the region of the pointed mountain peaks. We are held spellbound by these familiar forms on an outsize scale, the heterogeneous nature of which exerts an irresistible fascination. Spitsbergen is incomparably more majestic than the mountains, the fells, and the fjords of Norway.

Spitsbergen's Treasures

In the course of the earth's history, layer after layer was deposited on Spitsbergen, and we find repeated traces of life. There are carboniferous rocks which date from the Carboniferous, the Neocomian, or Lower Cretaceous, and most abundantly, in the strata of the Tertiary, where Arctic conditions have turned lignite into a glittering, highly petrified exploitable coal. It is a never-ending source of amazement to find magnificent, large, fossilized lime-tree leaves in this treeless Arctic latitude. The conclusion would seem to be that the climatic conditions here must in earlier times have been other than they are today. The credit for the discovery of Spitsbergen coal is due to the American Longyear. Since then, Norwegians and Swedes, Americans and Dutchmen, Englishmen and Russians have exploited this coal, and Norwegians and Russians continue to do so in various places today. At Barentsburg, Grumantbyen, and Pyramiden, a team of Russian miners dig for the black gold, and at Longyearbyen, Ny-Ålesund and Sveagruva it is mined by the Norwegians themselves.

However, it was not originally owing to the coal that Svalbard, uninhabited for centuries and bearing no traces of any ancient habitation, first became the home of a population which may best be described as a collection of short-term or long-term visitors. In earlier times, its other riches had already enticed intrepid men, who visited the group of islands as hunters.

First of all there was the abundance of sea creatures which attracted them. In 1607, Hudson, an English sailor in the service of the Dutch, brought the first whales and walruses home from the polar regions. The hunters soon swarmed over the Arctic during the brief summer, and Spitsbergen served as their most important base. In a short time, a Dutch trapper-station, called Smeerenburg, was established on the northwest corner of the island, and for a time it boasted more inhabitants than did Batavia! Apart from the Dutch, the British, Russians, Swedes, and Norwegians participate in this hunting enterprise, which will result in the total or partial extinction of the walrus and the whale respectively. The seals, too, have already been decimated. This is all quite understandable, however, when one remembers that every part of these aquatic mammals is utilized: the meat, the blubber, the oil, the skeleton and the horny plates of the whale (whalebone), as well as the tusks of the walrus and the skin of the seal, whose flesh, incidentally, is regarded as a special delicacy. In addition to this, the plentiful fish were, and still are, exploited. Fortunately, the cod, herring, halibut, salmon, and polar shark are so prolific that all this fishing activity has not seriously reduced their numbers.

There is also an abundant wild bird life there. The bird colonies on the Arctic cliffs may justifiably be called 'metropolises' in comparison with the more modest ones in Norway. The most famous are probably those on Bear Island, which lies midway between Norway and Spitsbergen, and, apart from birds, is inhabited by no living creature. There is surely nothing which bears more impressive witness to the utter peace of these polar regions than the excited fluttering of hundreds and thousands of birds startled from the quiet security of their cliff abodes on the approach of men. Then ensues a cawing and a croaking, a squawking and a chirping, up and down the scale, and at every conceivable volume, on the part of uncountable species of gull, stormy petrels, red-beaked puffins, black and white auks and guillemots; the greatest commotion is raised by the flocks of fast-fluttering little terns.

Web-footed birds and waders bring us out of the skies and down to earth again. Finally we turn our attention to the rather scanty fauna of the country, the representatives of which exhibit all kinds of singularities. Mammals with long and beautiful coats soon lured the hunters of fur-bearing animals, and they snared the dangerous polar bear, as well as the elusive Arctic fox. Musk-oxen and reindeer, however, are extremely rare on Spitsbergen and are therefore not hunted as game. On the whole, one has the impression that the profusion of sea and air fauna makes up for the lack of other wild life on the mainland.

Spitsbergen's Position on the Route to the North Pole

Spitsbergen is the northernmost site of human habitation in the Arctic Ocean. With complete justification, the coal-mining township of Ny-Ålesund on Kongs Fjord is called the most northerly community in the world. Not far from here the Swede, S. A. Andrée, set off on the balloon flight from which he was never to return. Amundsen and Ellsworth took up quarters here when they launched their offensive against the Pole by aeroplane in 1925, followed a year later by a second and successful attempt in the semi-rigid airship 'Norge'. It was here, too, that Byrd took off in the summer of 1926 and flew over the Pole in a Fokker two days before Amundsen. Nobile's 'Italia' also set sail on her ill-fated venture from the same point on Kongs Fjord. Nobile and some of his companions were subsequently rescued, but the polar hero, Roald Amundsen, lost his life in an air-crash near Bear Island during the search for Nobile and his party. Now, Spitsbergen, and with it the whole of the Arctic, is entering upon a new phase of development. The 20th century has made a focal point of the island and the North Pole region, which were once so remote. The northern Arctic Ocean of latter-day geographers has become the Arctic Mediterranean, which lies at the intersection of the shortest routes of communication between the continents. November 15th, 1954, with its first civil airline linking the Old World and the New by the polar route, and the voyage of the atomic submarine 'Nautilus' under U.S. Commander Anderson in the year 1959 are events of more than merely symbolic significance.

What has remained unchanged in spite of the revaluation of the world situation is Svalbard's extreme climatic position on latitude 77°–81° north. A tundra vegetation is the utmost the island can produce. A compact carpet of plants is only to be found in the sheltered interior of the numerous deep fjords; on Is Fjord there is still grass, and Kongs Fjord and Kors Fjord have a carpet of dwarf willows, but in the north-west—on Danes Island and Amsterdam Island, for example—it is no more than a coating of lichen. Only a little farther north, the summer pack-ice zone already begins, and beyond that lie the congealed, frozen expanses of ice in the region of the Pole.

Living Conditions

Winter may well be called 'the long polar night', whereas in the tropics it is the nights that correspond to winter. A bewitching summer with pleasant temperatures is followed by the long, dark, and often bitterly cold polar night, a veritable kingdom of contrasts! Let us take a closer look at living conditions in the Arctic. On its outskirts, we are still in the region of the tundra vegetation. Where even the warmest month no longer reaches an average temperature of +5° Centigrade, the region of eternal snow, ice, and rock begins. But here there are still twenty species of seed-bearing plants that manage to flourish. What enables them to do so? Neither the annual temperature nor the winter minimum is the decisive factor but, above all, the temperature reached during the summer, and the duration of the vegetation period, which is directly dependent on it. In Spitsbergen this period covers the months of June, July, and August. During this season, continuous polar day reigns and, at the same time, the plants engage in uninterrupted assimilation activity under the intense ultra-violet radiation; the total amount of warmth generated in this short time also has a beneficial effect. All this helps to explain the almost explosive Arctic springtime, when eighty-six different flowering plants bloom in the course of four short weeks. The explanation of the more flourishing vegetation in the interior of the fjords and bays, as compared with that on the open sea-shore, also lies here: the more balanced ocean climate lowers the summer temperatures, shortening the period of vegetation.

The arctic desert thus extends far south along the west coast of Spitsbergen and the fjords have the appearance of oases. The most amazing thing, however, must surely be that Spitsbergen's flowers are taller than its trees! A polar poppy *(Papaver nudicaulis)* in full bloom often attains a height of 6 inches, while the tiny stems of the dark green polar willow *(Salix polaris)*, which intertwine to form spreading carpets, are barely two inches above the ground; and yet, on closer examination, these stems prove to be of wood, with as many as thirty annual rings. Thus we have this diminutive tree growing side by side with plants and grasses only a year old, yet three times its height. The true polar climate is no better disposed towards man than it is towards trees, even when it assumes its mildest form, as it does on Spitsbergen. No one spends the whole year there unless he is obliged to do so, and this includes about two thousand Norwegian and Russian coal-miners, who are persuaded by attractive wages to continue working during the polar night. There are also a few stout-hearted trappers and hunters who know very well that, during Spitsbergen's winter, they can get certain otherwise elusive animals in their line of fire just in front of their log-cabins on the coast. In summer they would be obliged to comb the distant and inaccessible interior or the floes of the receding pack-ice to find these same creatures.

Quiet and reserved, the Norwegians stand at the rails when the time to leave actually arrives. One waves to those who are staying behind in Longyearbyen, one sends a final word of greeting to the men at the meteorological station on Cape Linné at the mouth of Is Fjord. Spitsbergen recedes, sinking slowly below the horizon of the Arctic Ocean and becomes no more than a lingering memory of a country unique in its formation and wondrous in its colours, shimmering silver in the magic light of Arctic summer days.

Werner Kuhn

Captions

1 Landmarks of the capital: Town Hall and training-ship, homeland and distant shores. Today Oslo has nearly half a million inhabitants; like Bergen, Stockholm, Helsinki, and Leningrad, it lies close to the 60th parallel. The Town Hall, built of red brick by Arnstein Arneberg and Magnus Poulsson in 1950, contains many treasures. The mermaid figure-head on the proud sailing-ship, *Christian Radich,* is looking towards Bygdöy, where the old Viking longships, Nansen's *Fram,* and Heyerdahl's raft, *Kon-Tiki,* rest after their long voyages.

2 An old sailor always hears the call of the sea. Behind him towers the ancient stronghold of Akershus, which used to protect the harbour entrance. Haakon V, the successor of Magnus Lagaböter (who is shown on the seal on p. 6), began its construction at the end of the 13th century.

3 See text to Plate 5.

4 Bergen can be reached overland by train, which passes round the 1,200 m. (c. 3936 ft) Hardangervidda, or by the scenically beautiful Haukeli Road, which first skirts the southern flank of the desolate Vidda to Hardanger Fjord, and then continues from Odda to Bergen (cp. Plate 60). Although the town lies further north than Cape Farewell in Greenland, the winter temperatures seldom drop below freezing.

5 Plates 3 and 5 show state-rooms in Bergen's Hanseatic 'court', dating from the beginning of the 18th century. Plate 3: between table and window, a small alcove-like private counting-house; dried cod suspended from the ceiling were thought to bring good luck. Today, Norwegian fishing-boats still carry them in the shrouds.

6 Bergen: view from the foot of Flöifjell (Photograph: Jack Brun, Mittet, Oslo). While large ships berth at the new quay further out, the fishing-vessels can sail in as far as Fiskebryggen in the inner harbour.

7 In the foreground, a Norwegian freighter; a daily Danish mail-boat is just steering its course between the skerries; since 1961, the Norwegian M.S. *Kronprins Harald* has maintained direct communication between Oslo and Kiel twice a week.

8 In the background, Ekeberg, with its school of navigation; ocean-going vessels set sail for distant lands from this quay.

9 Sailors of all nations praise the Norwegian beacons. The flash from the Mandal Lighthouse on Ryvingen, 7 km. (c. 5 miles) to the south of the town, can be seen 20 sea-miles across the Skager Rak in the direction of Jutland. The oldest Norwegian beacon stands 26 km. (c. 17 miles) to the west of Ryvingen, on the mainland, near Cape Lindesnes. The white tower, which is visible for miles even during the day, dates from the year 1915; but already in the days of the ancient Vikings, fire signals were given from here, and a beacon light has shone out from Lindesnes continuously since 1725 (cp. Plate 69). The most southerly point on the Norwegian mainland, Cape Lindesnes, lies at latitude 57° 58′ 43″ N., that is, further north than the northern border of the United States. Its name is familiar to most Norwegians, and to them 'our whole country' means 'from Lindesnes to the North Cape'.

10 Loshavn, 17 km. (c. 10 miles) north-west of Lindesnes, was important during the Napoleonic Wars, 1807 to 1814, as the outer harbour of Farsund. At that time, the harbour-town had 180 inhabitants; in 1900 there were still 130, while today, only 60 people live in Loshavn, and they are engaged mainly in fishing.

11 A southern summer paradise, one of many. The natural channel, which has been extended as a short-cut to the town of Kragerö, which is situated further west, today serves mainly the relaxation of holiday-makers (cp. Plate 71).

12–14 Of the former 750 stave churches, only 25 remain today. Heddal (Hitterdal) was completed in the year 1250, when the side-chapels were being built round Notre-Dame in Paris. After an unfortunate renovation in the years 1849 to 1851, Heddal's original appearance was later restored. The old Norwegian stave churches were generally surrounded by a low cloister, where the church-goers deposited their weapons.

Plate 13: the inner gallery of the age-blackened church at Borgund, which, judging by some runic inscriptions, is a hundred years older than Heddal. The round columns in the interior (Plate 14, Urnes) resemble the masts of a ship, and the gable-beams, with their dragon's-head ornamentation, are like the prow of a boat. The whole has been decorated by wood-carvers with elaborate designs of intertwined bands, dragons, and plant motifs, the profounder meaning of which we have perhaps not yet fathomed.

15 While the stave church at Borgund was under construction, Norwegian master-builders laid the foundations of the vast round limestone pillars of the Abbey Church of Hamar, four of which are still standing today. Breakspeare, the English-born apostolic nuncio, later Pope Hadrian IV, made an excellent choice of the site for the town and its cathedral on the shores of a deep-blue lake, upon which we look down from Hedmarkstoppen (cp. Plate 21).

16 17th century pulpit in St. Mary's Church, Bergen.

17 In the year 1150, Trondheim Cathedral was enlarged. In 1328, the church erected over the grave of Saint Olaf, the Mother Church of Norway, where coronations have been held since 1814, was ravaged by a serious fire; in 1432 it was struck by lightning, and in 1531, together with the town of Trondheim, it again fell a prey to the flames. In 1869, Norway began to reconstruct and extend, in accordance with old plans, this edifice, the most venerable of the Scandinavian Middle Ages. In the year 1930, on the 900th anniversary of Saint Olaf's death, the cathedral was re-consecrated.

18 Old warehouses, or storage-houses, built upon piles in the Nidelv, which generally remains free of ice, even in winter, in spite of the fact that Trondheim lies farther north than Labrador (cp. Vardö, Plate 39).

19 Nidaros, with its red-tiled roofs and winding streets, reminds one vividly of Lübeck or of the Nuremberg of Albrecht Dürer.

20 The Norwegian must struggle hard for his daily bread on the mainland, which is only 2.7% arable. Even in summer, the animals in our picture feel the icy breath of the mighty glacier.

21 With its delightful lakes, Hedmark is one of the few Norwegian provinces with lush meadow-lands, which provide pasturage for herds of the finest pedigree cattle.

22 This lake, 28 km. (c. 17½ miles) long and with depths of as much as 215 m. (c. 705 ft), is the largest in Jotunheim, covering an area of 18 square miles. In the foreground, one of the characteristic Norwegian stone 'signposts', or cairn-like landmarks.

23 Gulls nesting on the rugged cliffs of Svaerholtklubben, between Porsanger Fjord and Lakse Fjord, North Cape and Nordkyn.

24 Young sheep at an altitude of 3337 ft on the frozen Djupvatn, not far from Geiranger.

25–26 Since electricity is now supplied by enormous generators in modern power-stations (cp. Plate 45), wood is no longer used for fuel in Norway. The transport of the heavy tree-trunks to the saw-mills, wood-processing works, and cellulose-factories is partly by water and partly by lorry.

27 Hurricanes from the sea near by, landslides, and avalanches make it impossible for big trees to grow in this wild ravine.

28 Old bridges in Norway were generally built exclusively of wood. This mill (on left) is still worked by the running water in the age-old way. Norway is one of the richest countries in Europe as regards water-power, and the figure for the electricity generated *per capita* of the population is the highest in the world.

29 Lilac in flower near Ullensvang, on Hardanger Fjord.

30 Spring in the air on a mountain-lake between Stryn and Geiranger.

31 Farmsteads on Hedals Fjord in Oeystre Slidre (Valdres).

32 On Ese Fjord, a branch of Sogne Fjord.

33 Although Norway has a short summer, the sun shines longer there than in more southern latitudes. Already in heathen times the sun was worshipped, especially on that midsummer night when its soft light never quite leaves the sky, both in the south of the country and here at Farsund. The young folk celebrate this festival with singing and dancing.

34–36 Whether it is a warehouse on the coast or a small farmstead with its store-houses (= *stabbur*) on the shores of Lake Totak, in Rauland, there is always a pleasing harmony of material, form, and purpose. Plate 35: Alcove in the parsonage in Maihaugen Park (open-air museum) at Lillehammer, at the entrance to Gudbrandsdal.

37 Ålesund: 'Linefisker' with rubber floats for securing the nets and lines in the water. At the height of the herring-

fishing season, Ålesund often accommodates hundreds of fishing-cutters, round which screeching flocks of eternally hungry gulls circle and swoop (cp. Plate 47).

38 The *Havdun,* only 21 ft long. Norway registers more than 42,000 such coastal fishing-boats, 25% of which have their home ports in Möre and Romsdal, two regions in the west of the country.

39 Vardö lies on the same meridian as Cairo, about 200 km. (c. 120 miles) north-west of Murmansk. Here Fridtjof Nansen set off on his memorable polar expedition on July 21, 1893 (cp. text to Plate 1). The fishermen's settlement, which today has 3,500 inhabitants, was rebuilt after the Second World War, as may be seen from the new piles and trim warehouses on the waterfront.

40 Hammerfest is the most northerly town in the world, and lies to the west of the North Cape, at latitude 70° 40′ N., where the sun does not set from May 14 to July 28, nor rise from November 21 until January 23 (cp. Plate 69).

41 In the background, the Fjellstua, 135 m. (c. 443 ft) in height, on the Aksla. In 1904, the houses of Ålesund, built almost exclusively of wood, went up in flames (cp. text to Plate 17).

42 On visiting a Norwegian filleting-centre, one is struck by the scrupulous cleanliness of the factory. Even the smell of the fish-products, which are exported to all the countries of the world, is here subjected to a severe control.

43 Modern motor fishing-cutter at Bodö.

44 Narvik, with its ore-shipping quays. Day and night, trains laden with ore arrive from Sweden and pour their load through the cargo hatches of the vast ore-transport vessels.

45 Sarpsborg was founded by Saint Olaf in the 11th century; today it lies on the important railway line Oslo–Göteborg–Copenhagen–Continent. Near Sarpsborg, the Glomma, the longest river in Norway (611 km. = c. 380 miles), flows into the sea. Sarpsborg is capable of processing 18,000 tree-trunks a day, from which 1,100 tons of cellulose and paper are manufactured (cp. Plates 25 and 26).

46 Whalers still seek shelter from the Arctic storms in the skerries. Note the harpoon-gun in the bows and the crow's-nest on the foremast (cp. Plate 64, left).

47 Hungry gulls at midnight.

48 There is a great need of future sailors in a country with the second-largest merchant fleet in the world (cp. Plate 1).

49 The water in these small dockyards, which are scattered all over the country, is sufficiently deep for the building and repair of large shipping units. Majestic natural surroundings lend them special charm.

50 Nowhere do boom and depression alternate so rapidly as in tanker-shipping. These two laid-up tankers speak for themselves.

51 Richly-carved jib-boom of a training-ship in Tromsö harbour.

52 Fully dressed, M.S. *Oslofjord,* 16,500 GRT, has weighed anchor. A carpet of golden blossoms on the valley-floor contrasts with the snow on the peaks of the Geitfonnegga.

53 Typical Jotunheim scenery, where the snow-line lies 1,000 m. (c. 3,280 ft) lower than in the Swiss Alps.

54 Tongue of the Briksdalbree glacier.

55 In the course of technical development, industrialization will soon subject even this primeval landscape to a complete transformation.

56 Half-way between Gorsvatn (Plate 60) and Ullensvang (Plate 29); the water plunges 160 m. (c. 525 ft) into the Ringedalsvatn.

57 M.S. *Oslofjord,* the flagship of the Norway–America Line until the *Sagafjord* was taken into service (cp. text to Plate 8), has just passed the Syv Söstre (Seven Sisters) on the port bow. Since 1955, the Örnevegen (literally: Eagles' Path), which is 26 km. (c. 16 miles) in length and affords a wide view over the surrounding countryside, leads northwards from Maråk (Geiranger) to Ytredal.

58 Nearly all the ships of the 'Hurtigrute' Line were re-

conditioned after the Second World War and now sail under the flags of five different Norwegian companies.

59 This lake lies 20 m. (c. 65 ft) higher than Lake Bygdin (Plate 22) and its area is 4 square miles less. Its shores, like those of all the Jotunheim lakes, are desolate and uninhabited.

60 On the Haukeli Road from Oslo to Bergen, via Hardanger Fjord (cp. text to Plate 4), which is at present practicable only from June till October. Although it lies in southern Norway, the country surrounding the lake gives a truly Arctic impression.

61 'Ocean Viking', Norwegian oil and gas drilling station above 'Ekofisk' deposit in the North Sea.

62–63 For scenery, the country north of Trondheim can hardly be equalled anywhere in the world. At times it is a bizarre rock-formation that attracts the eye, at others a passing coastal motor-boat, and then again the fantastic scenery of Svartis massif (cp. Plate 68).

64/65 Tromsö, the turn-table of northern traffic. Excellent roads communicate with Narvik to the south, and with Hammerfest to the north. The largest town beyond the Arctic Circle, Tromsö, has become part of the mainland —the bridge, which is 1,036 m. (c. 1,133 yds) in length, was opened to traffic in the summer of 1960. It ranks as one of the greatest feats of Norwegian engineering.

66 A small wooden loading-ramp and S. S. *Fanaråken,* which, in spite of so much rationalization elsewhere, still do duty in the interior of Sogne Fjord.

67 Even heavy sightseeing buses are loaded in a few minutes on board the modern ferry-boats which are to be found all over Norway.

68 The Svartis massif, which extends southwards to the Arctic Circle over 174 square miles, covers an area as large as that of all the glaciers in the Bernese Oberland put together.

69 Beacon in the dangerous outer skerries of Hammerfest.

70 Naerödal, a continuation of the river-like Naerö Fjord, is often a mere 200 m. (c. 218 yards) wide. On the left, the blunt mountain-cone, 936 m. (c. 3,070 ft) high, of the Jordalsnut, dominating the upper valley.

71 As the narrow waters of the skerry-strewn sea cannot be navigated by large passenger ships, the coast between Lillesand and Kristiansand has become a veritable summer holiday paradise.

72 View from Vardöhus, a stronghold built in about 1300; it used to protect not only the great Varanger Peninsula, stretching far out towards Russia, but also Finnmark, Norway's richest fishing-grounds after Lofoten (cp. Plate 41).

73 From Vardöhus to the southern stronghold of Halden it is about 1,500 km. (c. 937.5 miles) as the crow flies. Fredriksten fortress was built during the years 1661 to 1671, and protected the old trading-routes from Sweden, Denmark, and Germany. Charles XII of Sweden lost his life during the siege of the fortress in 1718.

74/75 Lofoten: lowering clouds over the skerries (cp. Plate 75); the same place a year later (cp. Plate 74). Anyone who wants to get closer to Trolltindan, the high rugged peak (1,000 m., which is about 3,280 ft), must hire a motor-boat at Svolvaer; small tourist vessels are forbidden to enter Troll Fjord on account of the narrow passages and the danger of falling stones. Having worked our way up through swamp and birch scrub from the landing-place at the inner end of Troll Fjord, we find ourselves amid magnificent primeval scenery. The mountain giants on Austvagöy, generally enveloped in mist, were once believed to be the dwelling-places of demons and other supernatural beings, and were avoided (cp. Plate 79).

76 Traces of the Scandinavian Ice Age, which came to an end in northern Germany about 20,000 years ago, in Scandinavia much later; morainic rubble, grit, and sand on the narrow island of Jomfruland (lit. Virgin Territory), only 7 km. (c. 5 miles) in length (cp. Plate 11).

77 A great Norwegian natural phenomenon, Saltström, near Fauske, 1,227 km. (c. 766 miles) from Oslo, can today be reached by train. With the alternation of ebb and flood, up to 18,000 million cubic feet of water flow seawards and into Skjerstad Fjord four times daily through a gully that is 31 m. (c. 102 ft) deep and 150 m. (c. 492 ft) wide. At the spring-tide, the difference between high and low water is 3 m. (c. 10 ft), the rate of flow being as much as 28 sea-miles per hour, which corresponds to the travelling-speed of the most modern

160,000 h.p. fast steamer. The profusion of fish in Saltström makes it an El Dorado for anglers.

78 Tussock-grasses make the Saltström difficult of access.

79 On Lofoten Island (cp. text to Plates 74/75).

80 The North Cape massif, 300 m. (almost 1,000 ft) in height, consists of grey-black, cracked and rutted slate, and lies on the island of Mageröy. The most recent measurements have proved that Knivskjellodden, 4 km. (just less than 3 miles) further west, is the northernmost point in Norway (71° 1′ 18″ N.). The most northerly point on the continental mainland is Nordkyn headland, which is situated at latitude 71° 8′ 1″ N. and longitude 27° 40′ 9″ E., 68 km. (c. 42½ miles) further east than the North Cape itself, traditionally thought to be the northernmost point.

81 On the north-east point of Mageröy, thrust far into the open Arctic Ocean, Helnes is an important beacon for ships entering Porsanger Fjord. From April 25 to August 11, all the beacons on the Finnmark coast are extinguished, for during this time the midnight sun is shining, and at the North Cape it does not set between May 14 and July 30.

82 The North Cape is connected with Honningsvåg in the south-east of Mageröy by a road which was opened in 1956 (see text to Plate 58). In the foreground, the luxury yacht *Stella Polaris.*

83–85 Photographs taken in winter by Christian Doehler, Stuttgart (83: Going to church, 84: Mother and child, 85: Separating the reindeer). The pictures take us to Karasjok, not far from the Finnish border. If we exclude the Soviet Union, Karasjok probably has the lowest annual temperatures in Europe. For about 200 days in the year the mean temperatures remain below freezing-point, and temperatures of —51.4 °C. have been registered.

86 On the way from Revsborn to Smör Fjord and Russenes. The wooden *klubba* round the watch-dog's neck is to prevent him from running away.

87 The midnight sun, shining through a sufficiently thick veil of haze, gives rise to a fabulous interplay of lights and colours.

88 Whaler amid pack-ice at the entrance to Is Fjord during the polar night.

89 Another phenomenon, that of aerial reflection or mirage, can frequently be observed in Spitsbergen waters in the summer. Here a pack-ice edge has undergone such upward distortion that it appears like a high glacier front. Sometimes entirely flat islands, viewed from the distance, seem to have been raised into vast steep plateaus.

90 At latitude 79° 34′ N. we have reached the northernmost point of our journey. The Alkekongen, 814 m. (c. 2,672 ft) in height, is named after the innumerable auks which nest there.

91 Kongs Fjord is less blocked by ice in winter than the more southerly Is Fjord, and is therefore of greater importance to shipping (cp. Plate 88). Kongs Fjord was also the point of departure for most of the polar expeditions: in 1926 it was the airship *Norge,* captained by Amundsen, who crashed and lost his life while attempting to rescue the airship of his Italian colleague, Nobile.

92 Colliery in Ny-Ålesund, on Spitsbergen.

93 Longyearbyen is the largest permanent Norwegian settlement in Spitsbergen. Most of the coal mines are situated on the Ice Fjord; into this, from the South, runs a lateral valley and on its flanks stand the groups of miners' houses. The centre of the valley is not habitable, because a turbulent river rushes down it in summer. Nevertheless, the whole valley supports what is, for Spitsbergen, a dense vegetation, even on the mountains in the background it climbs up to nearly 1000 feet.

94 The wild reindeer is the biggest native land animal of Spitsbergen and is similarly content with its meagre diet of moss tundra. Compared with the Lapland reindeer, the Spitsbergen breed is a little smaller but much sturdier, and is distinguished by an enormous pair of antlers borne by the female as well as by the male. Though decimated in West Spitsbergen, the reindeer are still numerous in the eastern islands; their total number in the Svalbard archipelago has been estimated at a few thousand. They must have got to Spitsbergen, after the Ice Age, during the early summer following severe winters, across the ice bridges which then extended from Novaya Zemlya via Franz Josef Land. Their shed antlers are frequently found.

95/96 In those spots where running water washes down nutritive substances, where a boulder offers protection against the icy wind and stores up a little warmth on its southern side, or under a rock ridge where nesting birds provide an ample source of nitrogen, grow the few flowering plants of Spitsbergen—few in number but punctuating the wilderness with particularly brilliant splashes of colour. Their dazzling presence is the more puzzling to the naturalist as there are no insects about to perform pollination. Saxifrage and Arctic poppy, potentilla and catch-fly, and above all the large flower-heads of the exigeron—all these seem to have been put there just to delight the human eye. It is touching to watch these plants, whose flowers often push through the snow, trying to get their seeds to ripen during the brief 'non-summer' of barely 70 days. In this, they do not succeed every year.

97 Compact pack-ice within a solid field which has drifted down to the waters off Spitsbergen from the marginal zone of the polar sea. The hummocks in such a compressed field sometimes reach a height of 25 feet; at such points the ice sheet has a total thickness of up to 80 feet. The causes of compression are changes in wind direction, tidal currents and, above all, the resulting pile-up of ice sheets along the coasts. These processes affect mainly the marginal zone of the vast polar ice sheet; ice fields exhibiting such marked compression come into being especially in the polar sea north of Spitsbergen and Franz Josef Land. Deep inside the polar sea, in the vicinity of the North Pole, the absence of coasts and islands, and the much lesser effects of winds and tides, give rise to a much smoother surface of the ice. Its average thickness there is no more than 8 feet in the summer and 11 feet in the winter.

98 On the foreland of Neu-Bayerland (north-east edge of Edge Island) marine deposits rise to the 'marine line' with more than 100 beach ridges. This line shows that 10,000 years ago the sea level here was 250 feet higher (or, more correctly, the land lay lower) than today. In the middle distance on the right, the Freeman Glacier.

99 An extensive fossil beach terrace at an altitude of 160 feet with some beautiful blue freshwater lakes. In the middle distance on the left lies the highest 'marine line' at 250 feet. In the background are the flanks of a slate mountain, polished perfectly smooth by sheet wash.

100 Only rarely is a solid pack-ice cover with evidence of strong compression encountered off Spitsbergen during the summer. The deep blue water in the foreground is a small ice-hole in the ice; the emerald pool in the middle distance contains fresh water. The sea ice gradually loses its salinity as the salt solutions concentrate in the ice and diffuse downwards. Thus the higher ice hummocks are entirely free from salt after about a year. Pure fresh water is, moreover, supplied by the snow which falls on the sea ice. The fresh water pools on the ice are a most welcome source of drinking and washing water for all ships in Arctic waters.

101 In the peak summer season luxury liners bring large numbers of tourists to the islands. If they are fortunate enough to get some really sunny days the contrast between the perfect luxury on board ship and the utter solitude of the Arctic scenery is in itself a memorable experience.

102 Cape Linné on Is Fjord.

103 An air of complete remoteness and untouched purity hangs over the lonely rocky ridges which rise from the flat névés in the interior of West Spitsbergen — even when they are steeped in the rare brilliant light of the sun. The flat glacier bottom is frozen to a considerable depth and, compared with similar Alpine snowfields, shows little movement.